Cracking the Code

The Human Quest to Uncover Secrets

Rachel Kehoe

Illustrated by
Meegan Lim

ORCA BOOK PUBLISHERS

Published in Canada and the United States in 2025 by Orca Book Publishers.
orcabook.com

Library and Archives Canada Cataloguing in Publication
Title: Cracking the code : the human quest to uncover secrets / Rachel Kehoe ; illustrated by Meegan Lim.
Names: Kehoe, Rachel, author | Lim, Meegan, 1999- illustrator.
Series: Orca timeline ; 11.
Description: Series statement: Orca timeline ; 11 | Includes bibliographical references and index.
Identifiers: Canadiana (print) 20240478762 | Canadiana (ebook) 20240478770 |
ISBN 9781459839595 (hardcover) | ISBN 9781459839601 (PDF) | ISBN 9781459839618 (EPUB)
Subjects: LCSH: Cryptography—Juvenile literature. | LCSH: Ciphers—Juvenile literature. | LCGFT: Informational works.
Classification: LCC Z103.3 .K45 2025 | DDC j652/.8—dc23

Library of Congress Control Number: 2024946512

Summary: Part of the nonfiction Orca Timeline series for middle-grade readers, this illustrated book looks at the past, present and future of codes and codebreaking.

Orca Book Publishers is committed to reducing the consumption of nonrenewable resources in the production of our books. We make every effort to use materials that support a sustainable future.

Orca Book Publishers gratefully acknowledges the support for its publishing programs provided by the following agencies: the Government of Canada, the Canada Council for the Arts and the Province of British Columbia through the BC Arts Council and the Book Publishing Tax Credit.

Cover and interior artwork by Meegan Lim.
Design by Dahlia Yuen.
Edited by Kirstie Hudson.

Printed and bound in South Korea.

28 27 26 25 • 1 2 3 4

For my husband, Bas, my children, Isla, Rose and Rhys,
and all those who find joy in unraveling mysteries.

Coding powers the technology we use every day. Whether we're unlocking secrets or creating apps and games, codes are everywhere.
JACOBLUND/GETTY IMAGES

CONTENTS

INTRODUCTION

Secrets can be powerful. The leaders of countries—presidents, queens and generals, among others—know this. They exchange secret messages that can change history. But there are risks. What if the messages fall into the wrong hands? This dilemma sparked the invention of codes and ciphers, special ways of writing so that only the intended readers could understand the message. A code swaps out a word or phrase for a different word, number or symbol. In a cipher, letters are replaced rather than whole words.

These mysterious hieroglyphs were used over 3,000 years ago on the island of Crete in Greece. Though carved long ago, no one has yet fully figured out what they mean.
DAN SHACHAR/SHUTTERSTOCK.COM

Over centuries, bright minds have created numerous secret methods of shielding messages from prying eyes. But there are also the codebreakers, people who strive to crack these codes and discover the secrets for themselves.

This contest between codemakers and codebreakers continues even now. Codes are all around us today and more important than ever. When you make a phone call or send a text, your words zip around the world, bouncing off satellites and passing through different computers. On this journey your messages could be easily ***intercepted***. But there's a way to keep these messages safe. Encryption is a way of scrambling information to protect it from being stolen. It's crucial for things like protecting credit card information on the internet or keeping your online chats private.

Message sent! Texting makes it easy to stay in touch with friends, share plans and chat instantly. Some messaging apps have special encryption features to keep your conversations private.
DANI LLAO CALVET/GETTY IMAGES

Secrets Beyond Words

Just like the secret codes in messages, our DNA holds mysteries about who we are and where we come from. It's another kind of code that scientists are learning to read and understand, one that will have an impact on how we study and treat diseases.

In the past and today, brilliant minds have been working at coding, but you might not know their names. Their work is often kept top secret to prevent the other side from uncovering their identities. Many were, and are, part of cryptography teams, their groundbreaking discoveries hidden. Their work shapes the world of global security and secrecy in ways we are only just beginning to understand.

Will there ever be a code that no one can crack? Or will codebreakers always find a way to solve the puzzle? Codes and ciphers have protected and puzzled us throughout history. Let's uncover how these secret messages have changed our lives and how they might shape our future.

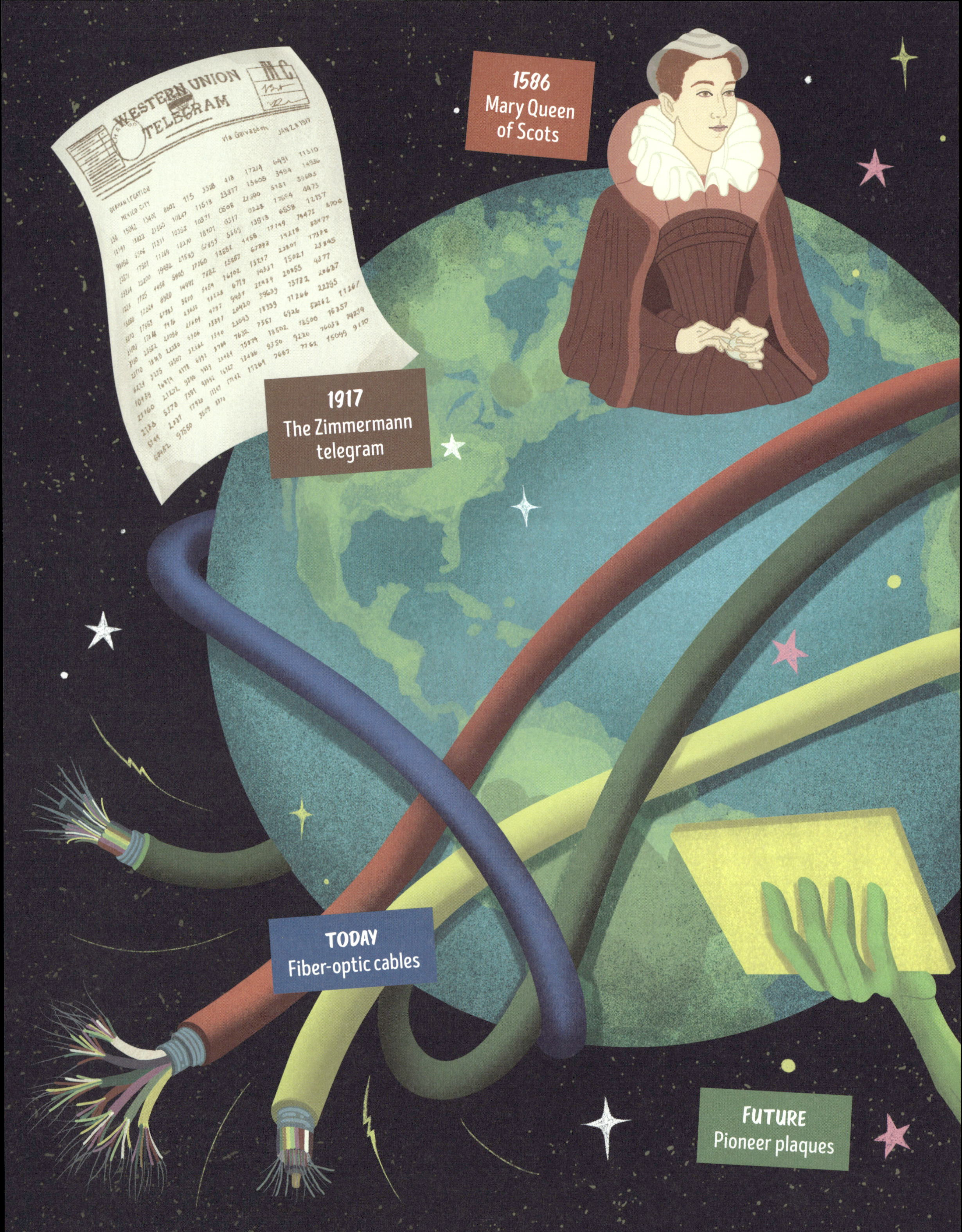
WESTERN UNION TELEGRAM
1586
Mary Queen of Scots
1917
The Zimmermann telegram
TODAY
Fiber-optic cables
FUTURE
Pioneer plaques

ONE

CODES THAT CHANGED OUR WORLD AND BEYOND

Throughout history, secret codes and ciphers have been at the heart of many major world-altering events. Cracking these codes has exposed the secret plans of both heroes and villains. These aren't just stories. These are true events where revealing a coded secret has changed, and can still change, the fate of political leaders and the outcome of wars.

Rival Queens

Mary, Queen of Scots

October 15, 1586

Fotheringhay Castle, Northamptonshire, England

On October 15, 1586, Mary, Queen of Scots, was on trial in an English courtroom, her future uncertain. She was accused of plotting to kill her cousin, Queen Elizabeth I of England. Sir Francis Walsingham, Elizabeth's secretary, was determined to prove Mary's guilt. He had captured other conspirators and was focused on exposing Mary as the leader of the plot. Elizabeth faced a tough choice. She didn't want to kill a queen, especially one who was her cousin. But ignoring a possible threat to her own crown would be risky.

WIKIMEDIA COMMONS/PUBLIC DOMAIN

Letterlocking

Back in the 16th century, keeping a letter private was a challenge. Paper was a valuable resource, and envelopes weren't common. People needed a clever way to ensure their words remained unseen by outside eyes. One creative solution was a system of cuts and folds known as letterlocking. A writer would start by cutting a slim strip along the margin of their letter. After writing their message, they would fold the letter into a compact shape, often a rectangle, and then punch a small hole through it. The strip was threaded through this hole multiple times, then tightly twisted, creating a "spiral lock." This method required no wax or glue. If someone broke this lock, the torn strip would show the letter had been opened.

DEUTSCHES BUCH- UND SCHRIFTMUSEUM/WIKIMEDIA COMMONS/CC BY 3.0

A QUEEN IN CAPTIVITY

Almost 20 years earlier, Mary had fled to England seeking safety from the fighting in Scotland. Her arrival offered hope to her supporters in England, who saw it as a chance to replace Elizabeth with Mary as England's queen. Elizabeth, sensing the growing support for Mary, kept her cousin confined in the countryside. This was a temporary solution, but soon Elizabeth's advisers suggested a permanent one—executing Mary.

A CODED CONSPIRACY

Walsingham, famous for his extensive spy network, suspected Mary of planning to take Elizabeth's throne. It was widely known that there was a plot to replace Elizabeth, but was Mary actually part of it? He needed solid proof, not just rumors. While Mary was imprisoned, she received secret letters of encouragement from her ***allies***. In July 1586, Anthony Babington, one of Mary's supporters, sent a letter telling her he had six friends who were eager to promote her reign and were ready to carry out a plan to execute Elizabeth and make Mary queen of England. Mary's response to Babington was quick: "Then shall it be time to set the six gentlemen to work, taking order upon the accomplishment of their design."

This became known as the Babington plot. It was Mary's agreement to this plan that led to her downfall. The messages, hidden in things like beer kegs, were written in a code that turned words into ***symbols***. To most people they looked like harmless doodles. Mary believed that even if they were found, they couldn't be used as evidence against her because no one could read them.

THE FATE OF A CIPHER

However, Walsingham wasn't easily fooled. He managed to get hold of these coded messages. The task of decoding them fell to Thomas Phelippes, an expert codebreaker. If Phelippes could decipher Mary's messages, her involvement would be exposed. Phelippes worked on Mary's complex cipher. For many, it would have been impossible to crack. But not for him. Phelippes revealed the messages that described a plot to execute Elizabeth, signed by Mary. This was the crucial evidence Walsingham needed. Faced with this proof, Elizabeth felt she had no option but to have her cousin executed. On February 8, 1587, the royal conflict ended when Mary, Queen of Scots, was beheaded at Fotheringhay Castle. Mary's execution strengthened Elizabeth's position as queen, leading to a time of peace and stability.

The Babington Plot

Babington had created a complex cipher to hide his messages. It is called a homophonic cipher, where each letter of the alphabet is swapped out for a specific symbol. He used 23 symbols to replace letters and 35 additional symbols for specific words or phrases. There were also symbols to indicate repeated letters and meaningless symbols to throw off decoders. To make sure they could correspond, Babington had found a way to get Mary a copy of the codebook. But Thomas Phelippes, a skilled codebreaker, cracked this cipher by identifying the most common symbols and their likely letter equivalents.

THE NATIONAL ARCHIVES (UNITED KINGDOM)/WIKIMEDIA COMMONS/PUBLIC DOMAIN

AB FORCES NEWS COLLECTION/ALAMY STOCK PHOTO

The Art of Underwater Cable Tapping

In World War I, the British military found a way to gather secret information. They used special ships and divers to find underwater cables used for transmitting telegraphs. Then they attached a ***tap***—a small device made of metal and rubber—to the cable. The tap would pierce the cable's outer layer to connect with the inside wires. With the tap in place, British intelligence could secretly listen to enemy communications, intercepting messages without anyone knowing. Today we use advanced technology like fiber-optic cables for underwater messaging. But tapping into communication lifelines is still very much a part of modern spying.

The Zimmermann Telegram

Arthur Zimmermann, German Foreign Minister

January 1917

Germany to Mexico

In the winter of 1917 the world was at war. Europe was a battlefield, and countries were picking sides in what we now call World War I. The United States wanted to stay out of the war. Politicians hoped to keep the fighting an ocean away. But a secret message changed the course of history. It traveled across the Atlantic and brought the war closer to the United States.

A HIDDEN GAMBLE

Sending coded messages in war is always risky. In January 1917 a coded message from Germany reached politicians in Mexico. The message contained an offer: if Mexico attacked the United States, Germany would see that it got Arizona, New Mexico and Texas in return—lands it had lost to the United States almost 70 years earlier. Germany's aim wasn't for Mexico to defeat the United States but to distract it. By drawing the United States into a separate conflict, Germany hoped to keep American troops from joining the war in Europe.

THE BRITISH CONNECTION

Britain had cut off Germany's telegraph cables in the English Channel, so Germany often sent coded messages via neutral countries. Zimmermann's telegram was sent from Berlin to the German ambassador in Washington, DC, and from there it eventually was sent to Mexico. But unbeknownst to Germany and the United States, British spies were listening in. Codebreakers Nigel de Grey and Dilly Knox began decoding the Zimmermann telegram. Together they identified patterns and recurring symbols. Although they couldn't decode everything, they managed to infer key parts of the message.

British politicians faced a tricky situation. They needed to tell the Americans about Germany's plan without letting on that they were listening to American messages. Their solution? They pretended to find the telegram during a fake break-in at the Mexican telegraph office.

When the United States heard about it, people were furious. The idea of Mexico attacking them with Germany's help made the far-off war feel very close. This news was one of the events that spurred the United States into joining the war. Germany's plan had backfired. On April 6, 1917, the United States declared war on Germany. That decision was key to the allies winning World War I on November 11, 1918.

WESTERN UNION
TELEGRAM
GERMAN LEGATION
MEXICO CITY

Guided by lines of code, the space probes *Pioneer 10* and *Pioneer 11* became humanity's first messengers to the stars.
DRAGANAB/GETTY IMAGES

A Message to the Stars

Carl Sagan, Frank Drake and Linda Salzman Sagan

Pioneer 10 launched on March 2, 1972, followed by *Pioneer 11* on April 5, 1973

The Universe

The *Pioneer* plaques are humanity's way of trying to talk to the universe. Made by American scientists and artists, these gold-aluminum plates are on board NASA's *Pioneer 10* and *11* spacecraft. These spacecraft, launched in the early 1970s, are now far out in space, past our solar system. Their mission? To communicate with any extraterrestrial beings that might find them. The plaques show what humans look like, where Earth is in the Milky Way and when the spacecraft left Earth. This information is shown using a cipher that illustrates the properties of hydrogen, a common element in the universe that might be familiar to another advanced civilization.

SPACE MESSENGERS

So far no extraterrestrial has responded to these messages. The last contact NASA had with *Pioneer 11* was in 1995 and with *Pioneer 10* in 2003. By then *Pioneer 10* was more than 7 billion miles (11 billion kilometers) from Earth. The likelihood of the plaques being found by extraterrestrials may be slim, but if they are, they will show humanity's love of knowledge—and how we encrypt it.

Pioneer 10 zooms past the massive gas planet Jupiter, gathering important information along the way. Launched in the 1970s, it travels through space helping scientists explore our solar system and beyond, venturing farther than any spacecraft before it.
ERIK SIMONSEN/GETTY IMAGES

100 BCE
The Caeser Cipher

16TH CENTURY
The Vigenère Cipher

18TH CENTURY
The Pigpen Cipher

TODAY
ROT13 cipher

TWO

KEEPING SECRETS SAFE

Whether it's for tricking an enemy or just sharing secrets with friends, clever people have come up with many different codes and ciphers. You might think codes and ciphers are the same thing, but there is a difference between them. A code swaps out a word or phrase for a different word, number or symbol. In a cipher, letters are replaced rather than whole words. Both forms of encryption play an important role in cryptography—the art of secret communication.

The Caesar Cipher

Julius Caesar

100 BCE

Shift cipher

The Caesar cipher is one of the oldest known ciphers. The legendary Roman general Julius Caesar used it to send ***confidential*** messages during war. It allowed him to communicate securely with his generals and kept his secrets safe from enemies. Even if Caesar's enemies got their hands on the messages, they couldn't make sense of them. This cipher's secret lies in its "shift." It moves each letter in the message a set number of steps down the alphabet. When it reaches the end, it loops back to the beginning. This changes a regular message into a jumble of letters—unless you know the secret shift number.

Caesar's favorite shift was three steps to the right. For example:

Plaintext: A B C D E F G H I J K L M N O P Q R S T U V W X Y Z
Ciphertext: D E F G H I J K L M N O P Q R S T U V W X Y Z A B C

In this cipher, A turns into D, B into E and so on. Thus the word SECRET becomes VHFUHW.

Helmet on, ready for action! Roman soldiers were required to march up to 32 kilometers a day in full armor, building their legendary endurance.
AZMANJAKA/GETTY IMAGES

ROT13

Fast-forward to today. ROT13 is a popular online cipher similar to the Caesar. It's short for "rotate by 13 places," and it works by moving each letter in the alphabet 13 spots forward. This simple code is commonly used on the internet to hide things like movie spoilers or answers to puzzles. While it's easy to solve, ROT13 provides just enough of a barrier to prevent accidental reading of hidden information.

UNLOCKING CAESAR'S CIPHER

The Caesar cipher is ***monoalphabetic*** code. It is easy to use, but it does have one weakness. With only 25 possible shifts, someone could try each one until the right message pops up. This method of trial-and-error decryption is known as a ***brute force attack.*** But it wasn't until centuries later that the cipher's limitations were known and more complex encryption methods were created.

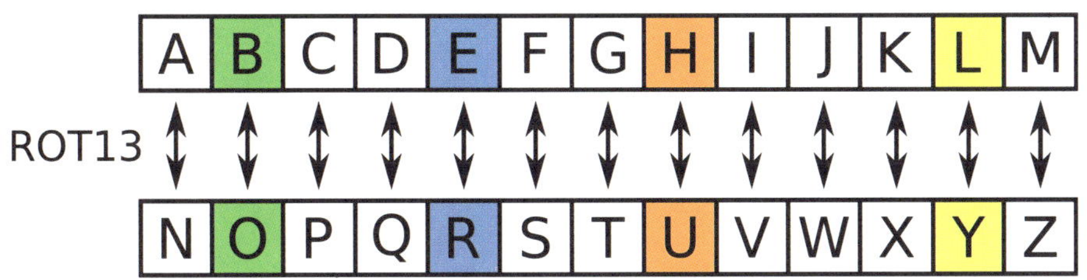

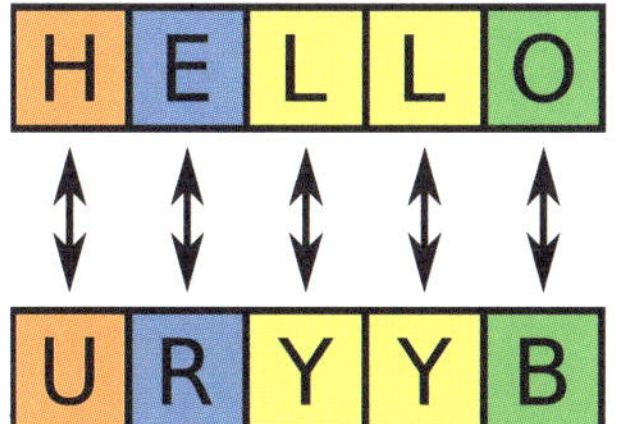

BENJAMIN D. ESHAM/WIKIMEDIA COMMONS/PUBLIC DOMAIN

What's the Frequency?

Around 800 years after Caesar, mathematician Al-Kindi spotted a flaw in the Caesar cipher. He observed that some letters, like *E*, show up more often in the English language than other letters do. By counting the number of times certain letters appeared in an ecrypted text, a technique known as ***frequency analysis***, he was able to guess the shift being used. For example, if *K* was common in the coded message, the shift was likely six steps, taking us back to the letter *E*.

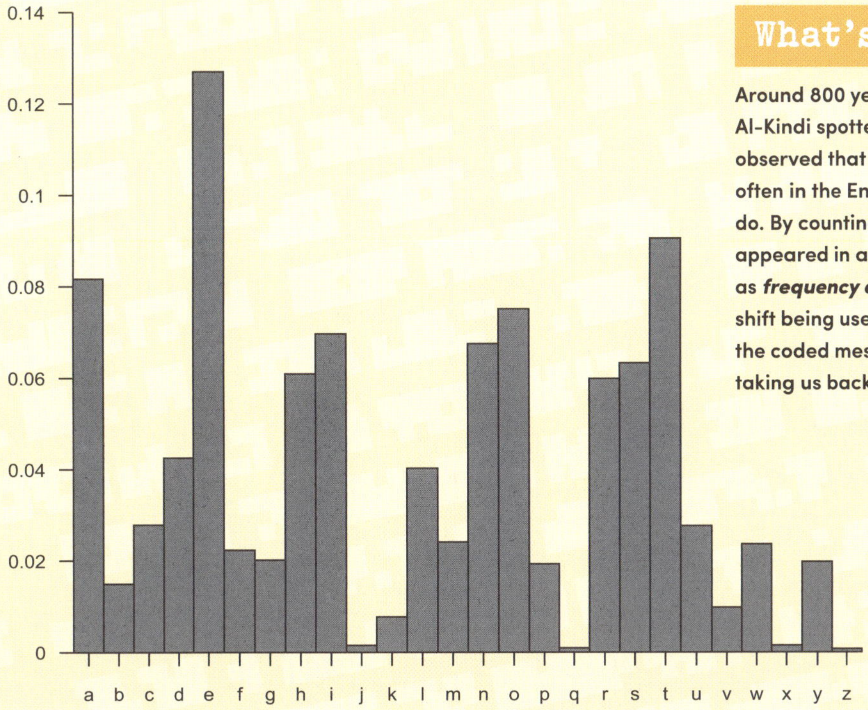

NANDHP/WIKIMEDIA COMMONS/PUBLIC DOMAIN

The Vigenère Cipher

Giovan Battista Bellaso	16th century	Substitution cipher

As codemakers got smarter, so did the codebreakers. The question was, could there be a truly unbreakable cipher? For about 300 years, it seemed the Vigenère cipher was just that. Despite being called the Vigenère cipher after Blaise de Vigenère, who devised a similar cipher in 1586, it was actually developed by Giovan Battista Bellaso. Pronounced *vidj-en-air*, it earned the nickname le chiffre indechiffrable, or "the unbreakable cipher," for its complexity.

Moving beyond the Caesar cipher's simplicity, the Vigenère cipher introduced a new element—the key. This is a word or string of letters that is repeated so that it matches the length of your message. Each letter in the keyword determines how you shift the matching letter in your message.

	A	B	C	D	E	F	G	H	I	J	K	L	M	N	O	P	Q	R	S	T	U	V	W	X	Y	Z
A	A	B	C	D	E	F	G	H	I	J	K	L	M	N	O	P	Q	R	S	T	U	V	W	X	Y	Z
B	B	C	D	E	F	G	H	I	J	K	L	M	N	O	P	Q	R	S	T	U	V	W	X	Y	Z	A
C	C	D	E	F	G	H	I	J	K	L	M	N	O	P	Q	R	S	T	U	V	W	X	Y	Z	A	B
D	D	E	F	G	H	I	J	K	L	M	N	O	P	Q	R	S	T	U	V	W	X	Y	Z	A	B	C
E	E	F	G	H	I	J	K	L	M	N	O	P	Q	R	S	T	U	V	W	X	Y	Z	A	B	C	D
F	F	G	H	I	J	K	L	M	N	O	P	Q	R	S	T	U	V	W	X	Y	Z	A	B	C	D	E
G	G	H	I	J	K	L	M	N	O	P	Q	R	S	T	U	V	W	X	Y	Z	A	B	C	D	E	F
H	H	I	J	K	L	M	N	O	P	Q	R	S	T	U	V	W	X	Y	Z	A	B	C	D	E	F	G
I	I	J	K	L	M	N	O	P	Q	R	S	T	U	V	W	X	Y	Z	A	B	C	D	E	F	G	H
J	J	K	L	M	N	O	P	Q	R	S	T	U	V	W	X	Y	Z	A	B	C	D	E	F	G	H	I
K	K	L	M	N	O	P	Q	R	S	T	U	V	W	X	Y	Z	A	B	C	D	E	F	G	H	I	J
L	L	M	N	O	P	Q	R	S	T	U	V	W	X	Y	Z	A	B	C	D	E	F	G	H	I	J	K
M	M	N	O	P	Q	R	S	T	U	V	W	X	Y	Z	A	B	C	D	E	F	G	H	I	J	K	L
N	N	O	P	Q	R	S	T	U	V	W	X	Y	Z	A	B	C	D	E	F	G	H	I	J	K	L	M
O	O	P	Q	R	S	T	U	V	W	X	Y	Z	A	B	C	D	E	F	G	H	I	J	K	L	M	N
P	P	Q	R	S	T	U	V	W	X	Y	Z	A	B	C	D	E	F	G	H	I	J	K	L	M	N	O
Q	Q	R	S	T	U	V	W	X	Y	Z	A	B	C	D	E	F	G	H	I	J	K	L	M	N	O	P
R	R	S	T	U	V	W	X	Y	Z	A	B	C	D	E	F	G	H	I	J	K	L	M	N	O	P	Q
S	S	T	U	V	W	X	Y	Z	A	B	C	D	E	F	G	H	I	J	K	L	M	N	O	P	Q	R
T	T	U	V	W	X	Y	Z	A	B	C	D	E	F	G	H	I	J	K	L	M	N	O	P	Q	R	S
U	U	V	W	X	Y	Z	A	B	C	D	E	F	G	H	I	J	K	L	M	N	O	P	Q	R	S	T
V	V	W	X	Y	Z	A	B	C	D	E	F	G	H	I	J	K	L	M	N	O	P	Q	R	S	T	U
W	W	X	Y	Z	A	B	C	D	E	F	G	H	I	J	K	L	M	N	O	P	Q	R	S	T	U	V
X	X	Y	Z	A	B	C	D	E	F	G	H	I	J	K	L	M	N	O	P	Q	R	S	T	U	V	W
Y	Y	Z	A	B	C	D	E	F	G	H	I	J	K	L	M	N	O	P	Q	R	S	T	U	V	W	X
Z	Z	A	B	C	D	E	F	G	H	I	J	K	L	M	N	O	P	Q	R	S	T	U	V	W	X	Y

BRANDON T. FIELDS/WIKIMEDIA COMMONS/PUBLIC DOMAIN

Word searches are similar to codebreaking—both involve spotting hidden patterns. The largest one ever made had an amazing 10,500 words and 129,600 letters! It holds the Guinness World Record for being the biggest word search puzzle ever made.
WESTEND61/GETTY IMAGES

THE STRENGTH OF THE SECRET KEY

The first step is to create a Vigenère square. The 26 letters of the alphabet make up the first row and the first column of the square. Starting in the second row, the letters shift to the left by one position (in a cyclical way, so that when A shifts to the left, it becomes the final letter of the second row). This shift continues with each subsequent row. The Vigenère cipher is ***polyalphabetic***, meaning it uses multiple shifted alphabets in a single message. This is what makes the code so strong.

To encrypt a message, you first choose a keyword. Let's use *tree*. To uncover the hidden message, the person receiving it must know the keyword. This keyword tells them which row of the Vigenère square to use for each letter of the message.

Let's say the message is *attack at dawn*. We need to match the length of the keyword to the message. In this case, the word *tree* is shorter than the message, so we repeat it until it is long enough. The repeated keyword would be *treetreetree*. This is known as the ***keystream***.

Using the Vigenère square and the keystream, we can now hide the message. The columns represent the letters of the keyword, and the rows represent the letters of the message. The point where a column and row meet gives us the hidden letter.

For example, our first keyword letter is *T*, and our first message letter is *A*. Where these intersect on the square gives us the first hidden letter, *T*. We do this for each letter to get the hidden message.

Original message:
ATTACKATDAWN

Key:
TREETREETREE

Ciphertext:
TKXEVBEXWRAR

UNVEILING VIGENÈRE

For a long time the Vigenère cipher was thought to be unbreakable. However, in 1854 Charles Babbage, an English mathematician, managed to crack it, though he never published his method. In 1863 Friedrich Kasiski also cracked it, and he shared his technique, now called the Kasiski examination. Later, in 1920, American cryptographer William F. Friedman developed the Friedman test, another solution to this once unbreakable cipher.

The Pigpen Cipher

Freemasons

18th century

Substitution cipher

Compared to the Vigenère cipher, the pigpen cipher is a simpler way to encode messages. Known for its unique and quirky setup, this cipher trades letters for symbols and uses a series of grids that look like pigpens, with dots representing the pigs. To the untrained eye, the intercepted message might look like playful doodles, but these scribbles actually hold the key to a hidden message. Here's what the pigpen grid looks like:

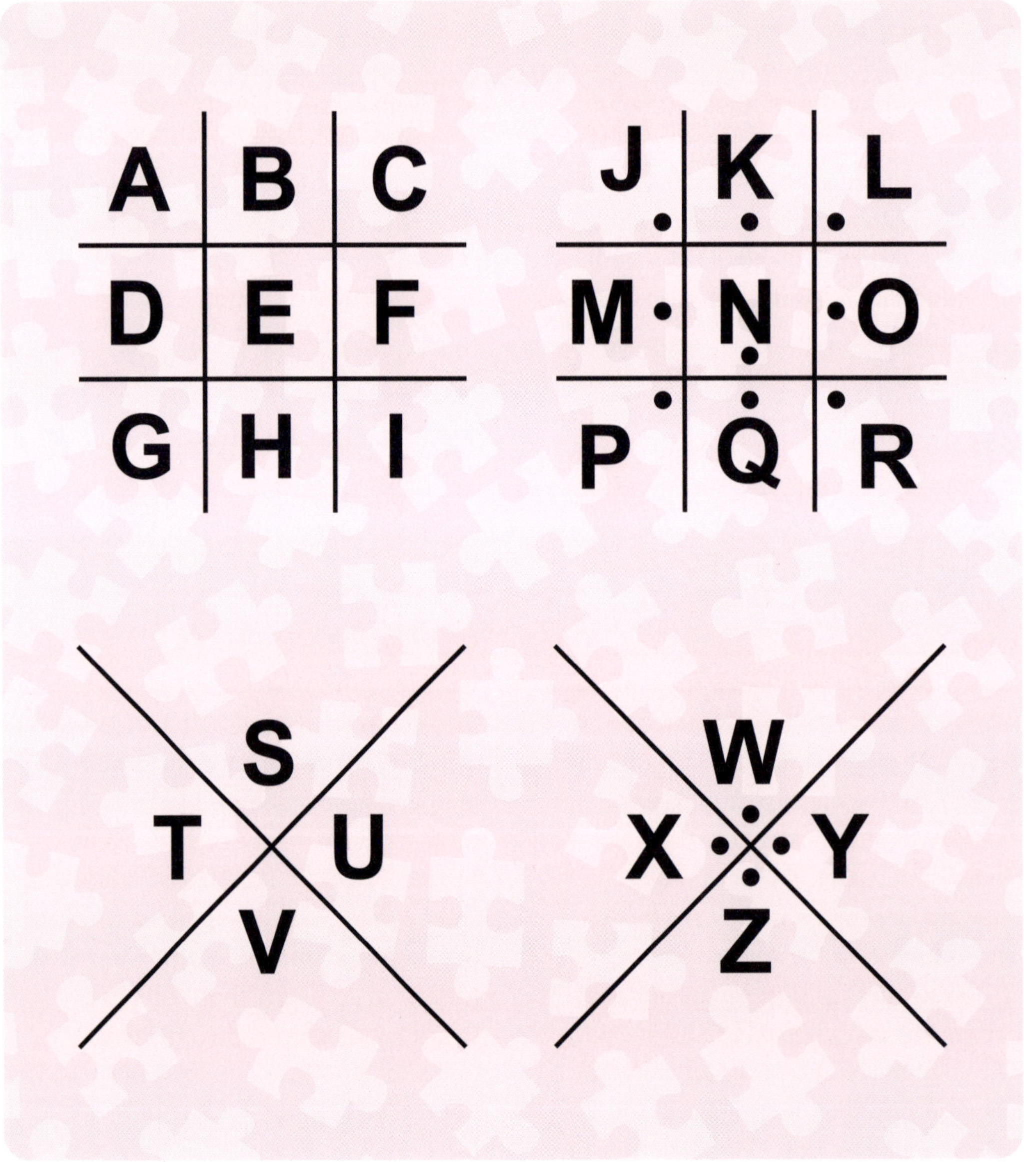

A	B	C
D	E	F
G	H	I

J	K	L
M	N	O
P	Q	R

S
T U
V

W
X Y
Z

ANOMIE/WIKIMEDIA COMMONS/PUBLIC DOMAIN

UNRAVELING THE MYSTERY

In the pigpen cipher each letter of the alphabet is swapped for a unique symbol, based on a grid of lines and dots.

The letter *A* turns into this symbol:

E becomes this:

N and *W* change to this:

This code lets you weave a hidden message in a pattern of symbols. Try decoding this example using the first example of the pigpen cipher:

A SECRET SOCIETY'S CODE

But who used this intriguing cipher? The Freemasons, a centuries-old secret society, are its most famous users. That's why it's also known as the Masonic or Freemason's cipher. The Freemasons began as stonemasons, skilled craftsmen who worked with stone, before becoming a brotherhood with their own secret handshakes, symbols and rituals. They adopted the pigpen cipher to keep their building techniques, design secrets and special symbols hidden from outsiders. Some of America's founding fathers, such as George Washington and James Monroe, were Freemasons, as were several Canadian prime ministers, such as Sir John A. Macdonald and John G. Diefenbaker.

While people don't use the original pigpen cipher much anymore, they still play with newer versions of it in games and learning activities. This shows that even when a code is cracked, it doesn't just disappear. Sometimes it changes and sticks around. Can you decrypt the answer to this riddle using the pigpen cipher?

I speak without a mouth and hear without ears. I have no body, but I come alive with wind. What am I?

Echoes from the Past

Trinity Church, right next to One World Trade Center in New York City, has a real-life example of the pigpen cipher. It's on the tombstone of James Leeson, who died September 28, 1794. His grave is decorated with well-known Masonic symbols, including a flaming urn, a winged hourglass and a compass. At the top of the grave are strange angular markings. Keen codebreakers identified these as part of the pigpen cipher. Decoded, these symbols spell out a stark message: *Remember Death*. It's a haunting use of a cipher that has lasted hundreds of years.

Freemasons use unique handshakes to show rank, such as Entered Apprentice, Fellow Craft and Master Mason. Each handshake marks a member's level in the organization and is used during official Masonic ceremonies.
PHOTOS.COM/GETTY IMAGES

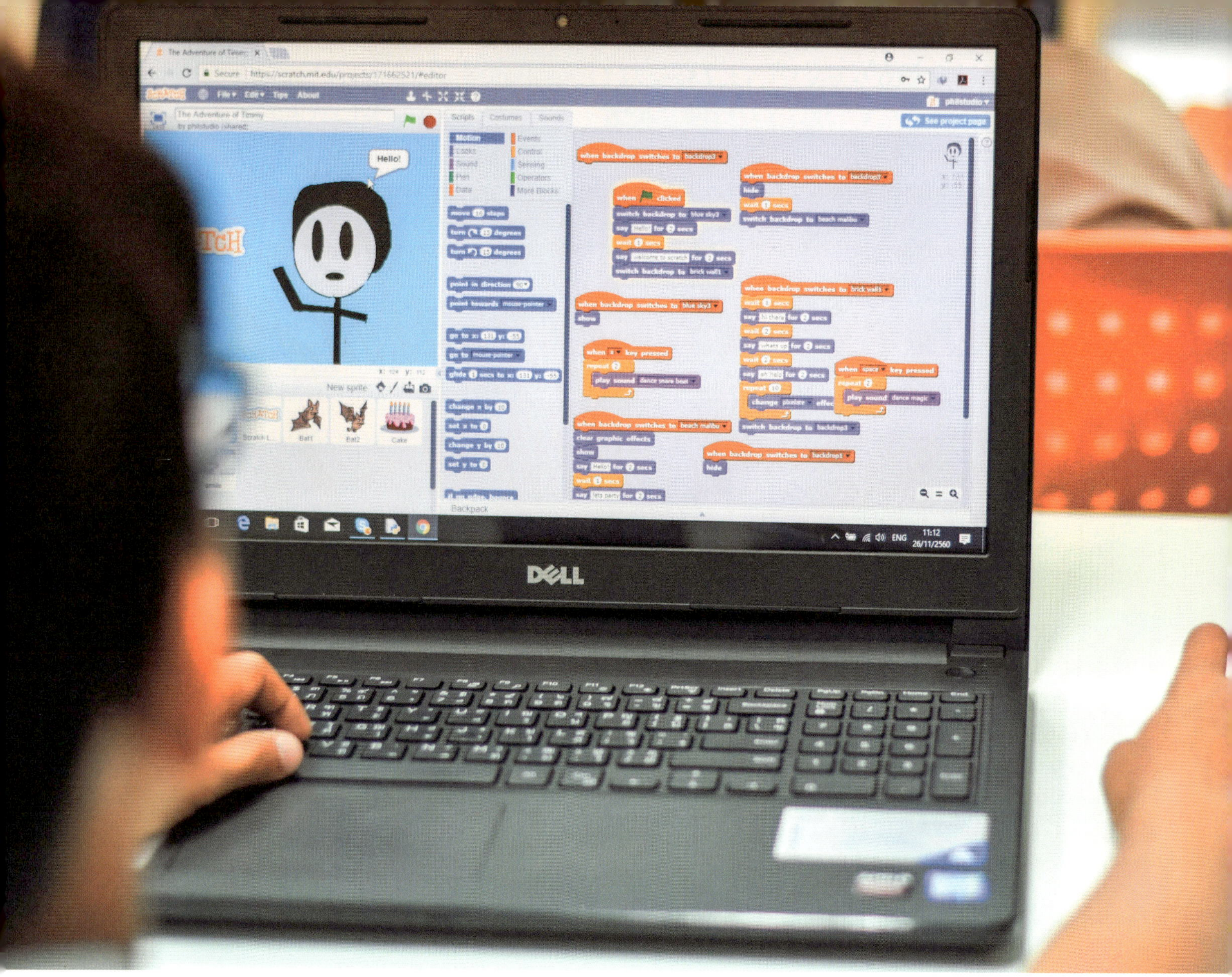

Snap blocks together and watch your ideas come to life! With Scratch, you can easily build games and stories by stacking commands that guide characters through fun, creative actions.
PHIL'S MOMMY/SHUTTERSTOCK.COM

Scratch: A Coding Playground

Mitchel Resnick, Yasmin Kafai and the MIT Media Lab	2007	Visual coding language

Today when we say the word *code*, we don't mean secrets scribbled on paper, waiting to be passed from hand to hand. We think of it as a language that tells computers what to do and that can be used for creativity and fun. Scratch is a visual programming language often used in schools to introduce young people to coding concepts. You can use Scratch code to build your own games and stories in a digital format.

SIMPLIFYING CODE CREATION

All video games run on code. Scratch makes coding easier with colorful blocks that snap together like puzzle pieces. Each block represents a different command, guiding you step by step. For example, to move a character in a game, you might start with a block that says *when flag clicked*. Next you would add blocks that say *move 10 steps*, *turn left* and *jump*. As you click the *flag* button, your character moves through these actions. This sequence of blocks forms a code that brings your game to life.

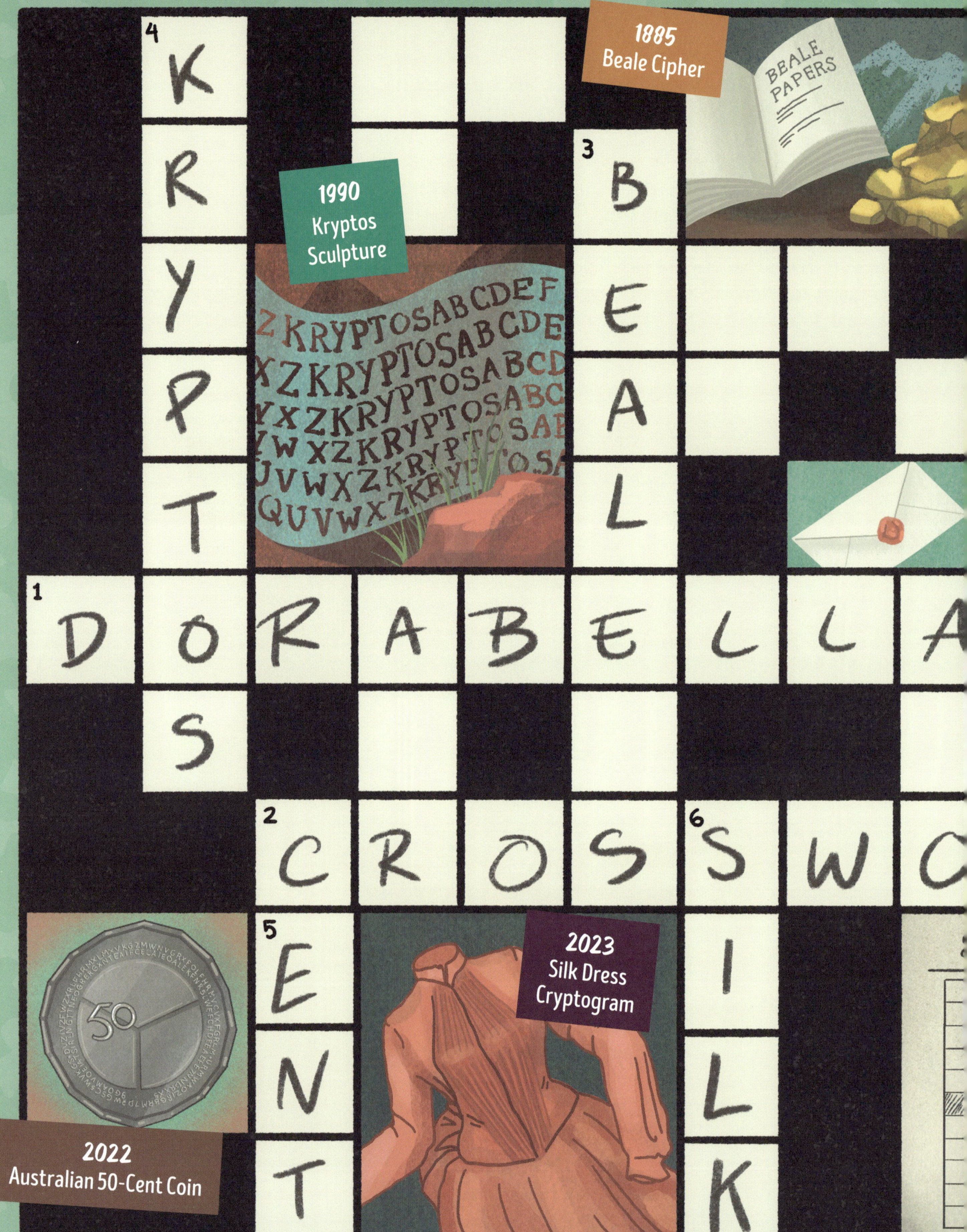
1885
Beale Cipher
BEALE PAPERS
1990
Kryptos
Sculpture
4 KRYPTOS
3 BEAL
1 DORABELLA
2 CROSSWO
5 ENT
6 SILK
2023
Silk Dress
Cryptogram
2022
Australian 50-Cent Coin

1897
Dorabella Cipher

1942
MI6 Crossword Puzzle

THREE

CODEPLAY

Codes make great puzzles. Symbols and letters become riddles where every sequence might unlock a mystery. Some codes are thought to be unbreakable, and people go to great lengths to crack them. Their dedication shows that making and breaking codes isn't just a skill—it's an exciting challenge for anyone with a curious mind.

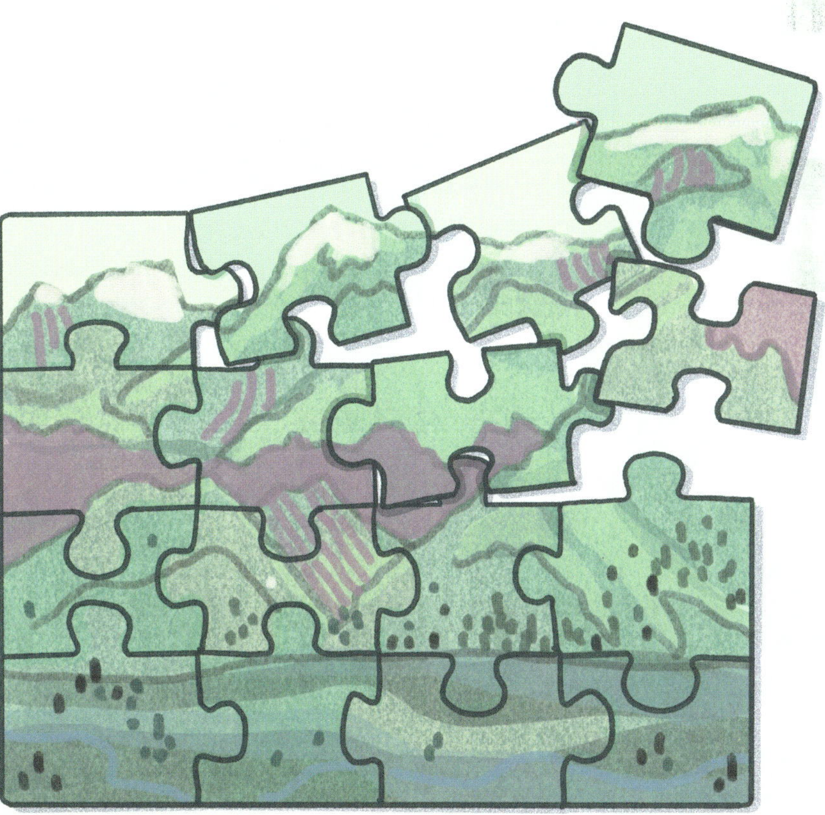

WIKIMEDIA COMMONS/PUBLIC DOMAIN

SEAN ANTHONY EDDY/GETTY IMAGES

The back of the Declaration of Independence has a handwritten note reading "Original Declaration of Independence dated 4th July 1776." No one knows who wrote it or why, adding a bit of mystery to this famous document.

Beale Cipher

Thomas J. Beale

1885

Bedford County, Virginia

A canyon slices through towering mountain ranges and stretches across the high plains near Denver, Colorado. It was in this rocky landscape, back in the early 1800s, that a band of 30 Virginians stumbled upon a hidden fortune. While on a bison-hunting expedition, the group's leader, Thomas J. Beale, discovered deposits of gold and silver. For about 18 months, the men mined the area, gathering a stash now thought to be worth a staggering US $43 million.

Restless for more adventure but worried about losing their fortune, the group decided to bury the treasure in the mountains near Bedford, Virginia. Beale transported the treasure himself. He created three ciphers that held clues about the treasure's location. He entrusted the ciphers to Robert Morris, an innkeeper in Lynchburg, Virginia, promising him that a decoding key would soon follow.

PASSED ON

Twenty-three years went by, but no word came from Beale. Many people thought he had died. Stumped by the ciphers, Morris passed them to a friend, James B. Ward. He had a breakthrough and solved the second cipher. Ward discovered that each cipher number in Beale's code matched a word in the Declaration of Independence.

This clue revealed a description and the general location of the buried treasure—about 4 miles (6.5 kilometers) from Buford's Tavern in Montvale, Virginia.

The last sentence of the decoded message reads, "Paper number one describes the exact locality of the vault, so that no difficulty will be had in finding it." In 1885, unable to solve the remaining two clues, Ward published the ciphers in a pamphlet called *The Beale Papers*. This sparked a global frenzy of codebreakers determined to find the treasure. But 140 years later, the mystery remains unsolved.

CHANGING FORTUNES

Beale's reasons for creating the ciphers are as unclear as the ciphers themselves. Was it a trick? Or did Beale actually want the treasure to be found? Among the treasure hunters attracted by the mystery over the years were brothers George Hart and Clayton Hart, who spent decades trying to decode the remaining ciphers, eventually giving up in 1952. There are also whispers that the ***National Security Agency (NSA)*** has taken a crack at finding the treasure. The only thing we know for sure is that one of the ciphers has been solved. That's what keeps this legend alive.

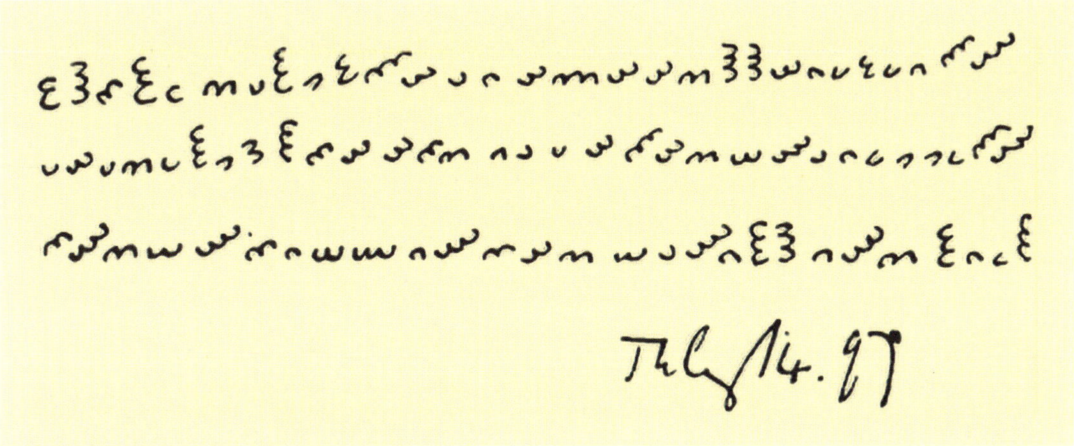

EDWARD ELGAR/WIKIMEDIA COMMONS/PUBLIC DOMAIN

Dorabella Cipher

Have you ever heard *Pomp and Circumstance*, the music you often hear at graduation ceremonies? Well, its composer, Edward Elgar, also created another masterpiece. But it isn't musical—it's mysterious. It's a message he wrote in 1897 for his young friend Dora Penny, whom he nicknamed Dorabella. This isn't your average letter. It's filled with 87 squiggly doodles that have left readers baffled.

Dora stashed the message away, unable to crack its code. Years later it resurfaced in her memoir, published in 1937. Elgar loved puzzles and riddles, and the one he sent to Ms. Penny has remained a mystery. No one has solved this cipher, not even codecracking pros. Some think it could be a cryptic hint about another of Elgar's works. Others believe it is a hidden inside joke between friends, but interest in solving it continues. The Elgar Society held a competition in 2007 to crack it, but no one succeeded. Whatever it says, the Dorabella cipher remains an unsolved riddle.

Kryptos

Jim Sanborn

November 3, 1990

CIA headquarters, Langley, Virginia

Nestled in the courtyard at ***Central Intelligence Agency (CIA)*** headquarters, a mysterious sculpture stands out. It's made out of red granite, wood and copper, and it forms a wavy S-shaped column. There are 865 characters carved onto this column—a mix of letters and numbers that make up four coded messages, each locked with a different cipher. Set beside a pool, the sculpture has a double purpose—it is both a work of art and a puzzle waiting to be solved.

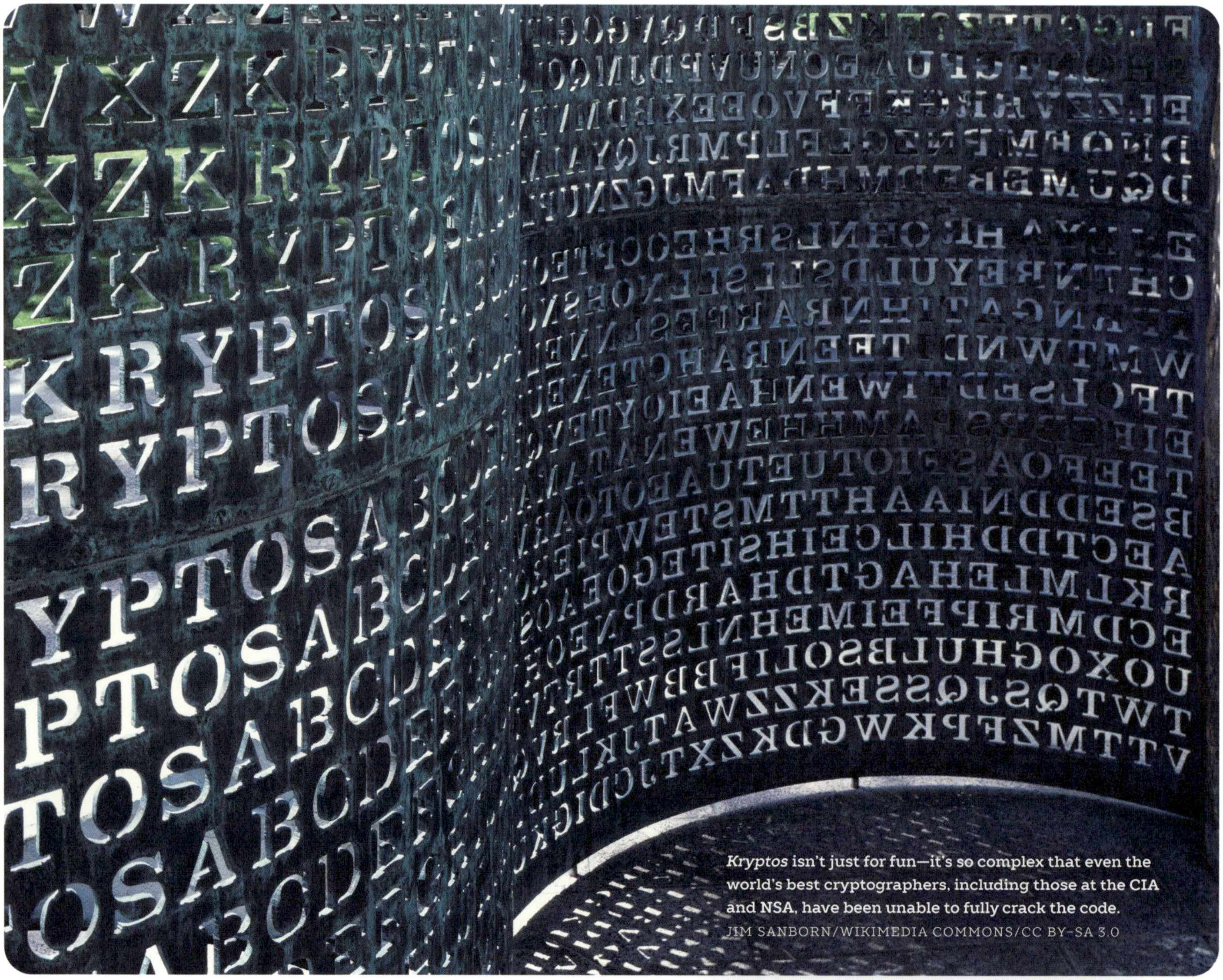

Kryptos isn't just for fun—it's so complex that even the world's best cryptographers, including those at the CIA and NSA, have been unable to fully crack the code.

Some mysteries, like the final part of the *Kryptos* sculpture, have puzzled people for years. They wonder if they can crack the code that no one else has solved.
UMNAT SEEBUAPHAN/GETTY IMAGES

AN UNSOLVED RIDDLE

The sculpture is named *Kryptos*, the Greek word for "hidden." Many of its secrets didn't stay hidden for long. In 1998 CIA analyst David Stein cracked three of the four messages. The following year, James Gillogly, a computer scientist, deciphered 768 characters of the fourth message, but so far the rest of the message has not been cracked. It's a challenge that keeps the best codebreakers guessing. The sculpture's creator, Jim Sanborn, worked with a retired CIA cryptographer for four months to design the ciphers. He wanted to be sure they were complex enough to challenge even the most skilled analysts.

A TRAIL OF CLUES

Over the years Sanborn has dropped three clues to help solve the fourth riddle. In 2010 he revealed the clue BERLIN. In 2014 it was CLOCK, and in 2020, NORTHEAST. These clues still haven't led to a solution for the remaining 97 characters of the fourth passage. It reads like this:

OBKRUOXOGHULBSOLIFBBWFL-
RVNORTHEASTOTWTQSJQSSEKZZ-
WATJKLUDIAWINFBBERLINCLOCK-
WGDKZXTJCDIGKUHUAUEKCAR

Cracking the four passages is expected to reveal a larger puzzle, and this has gathered unexpected attention. As people have solved parts of the *Kryptos* code, interest in the remaining mystery has grown, sparking discussions online, in articles and even in books and TV shows. This attention has turned *Kryptos* into a popular topic, reaching far beyond its original cryptographic audience. Sanborn is now thinking of selling the final clue and donating the money to climate research. *Kryptos* is a tantalizing challenge for codebreakers.

Coins aren't just for spending—they're made for cracking codes! Australia's 2022 50-cent coin challenges codebreakers with hidden messages, continuing a tradition of secretive designs found on coins throughout history.
NATASHA LAZARIDI/GETTY IMAGES

Australian 50-Cent Coin

Rachel Noble

September 1, 2022

Australian Signals Directorate (ASD), Canberra, Australia

Imagine cracking a riddle that leads to an interview for a job as a real-life codebreaker. Sound too good to be true? Not if you're in Australia. To mark the 75th anniversary of its spy agency, the Australian Signals Directorate (ASD), the government released a 50-cent coin. But this coin is far from ordinary. Hidden within its design are four layers of code, each presenting a challenge similar to what ASD experts face every day. The agency's director-general, Rachel Noble, says anyone who is able to solve them could be qualified for a job at the ASD.

HONORING CODECRACKING HEROES

The new coin celebrates Australia's history of codebreaking. During World War II, Australian codebreakers would intercept secret messages from the Japanese military and decipher them using a pencil and paper. They would then reencode these messages and send them to their allies, revealing the location of Japanese fighters. The coin also shows how far encryption technologies have come in 75 years, from simple paper-and-pen techniques to today's complex computer programs and secure ways to send messages.

As online ***cyberthreats*** increase, the ASD is actively seeking new talent—it aims to hire 1,900 more people to work at the spy agency. The coin is designed to catch the eye of future codebreakers and problem-solvers—a shiny invitation to those who excel at cracking codes.

The first person to solve the codes on the coin was a 14-year-old boy from Tasmania. His solution revealed the variety of codes on the coin, such as puzzles including simple letter reversals where A becomes Z, grids that rearrange letters to form messages, and more complex codes that mix up numbers and letters. It also has a modern ***binary*** code and Morse code to hide additional secrets in the design.

The clever use of codes on the coin not only showed the skills needed in modern cryptography but also served as a great advertising campaign for enlisting new codebreakers.

A Puzzle That Unlocked More Than Answers

The idea of using public challenges to find smart people for top-secret work isn't a new idea. On January 13, 1942, a British newspaper called the *Telegraph* ran a tough crossword puzzle. Readers who solved it in under 12 minutes were asked to contact the newspaper and were invited for a second, face-to-face challenge. What most people didn't know was that observers from MI6, the British Secret Intelligence Service, were watching the results. Being good at crosswords is a lot like being good at figuring out codes.

Four successful contestants were invited to meet with the government. Among them was Stanley Sedgwick, an accounting clerk, who stood out and caught the attention of the MI6 observer. Sedgwick received an invitation to go to Whitehall, an area known as the center of government in the United Kingdom. He was asked to sign the Official Secrets Act and was recruited to crack codes at Bletchley Park, the heart of British intelligence during World War II. This unusual way of finding clever codebreakers turned out to be successful, and codebreaking agencies stil use puzzles to try to attract candidates today.

Secrets in a Silk Dress

Wayne Chan, Sara Rivers-Cofield

2023

University of Manitoba, Canada

In 2013 dress collector Sara Rivers-Cofield bought a beautiful 1880s-era silk dress from an antique mall in Searsport, Maine. Little did she know this dress held a secret that would baffle codebreakers for nearly a decade. When she got home, Rivers-Cofield and her mother discovered two crumpled pieces of paper hidden in a secret pocket of the dress. The papers contained 23 lines of seemingly ***random*** words, including *Bismark Omit leafage buck bank.*

The strange lines puzzled Rivers-Cofield, so she shared them on her blog. The cryptic message quickly caught the attention of the global codebreaking community. Someone noticed it was telegraphic code. But for years it remained one of the world's top unsolved encrypted messages.

Throughout history clothes have hidden more than just style. During World Wars I and II, spies used knitting and hidden seams in clothing to conceal secret messages, smuggling valuable information past enemy forces without raising suspicion.
SARA RIVERS-COFIELD

POCKET OPENING

DRESS DECODER

In the late 1800s, telegraph codes were common, as the telegraph was the fastest way to communicate over long distances. Telegraph machines sent electrical signals over wires, transmitting messages in Morse code. Inventors and operators created thousands of codes, allowing a single word to represent a whole phrase or sentence. This made messages quicker and cheaper to send, and it also kept them private. Without the correct codebook, the messages looked like a meaningless series of words.

Wayne Chan, a research computer analyst at the University of Manitoba, was drawn to the mystery. He spent years poring over 170 codebooks and through archives and historical documents, trying to decode the cryptic message. What caught Chan's attention was how the silk-dress cryptogram resembled old weather messages from the 1800s. This clue led him to contact the archives of the National Oceanic and Atmospheric Administration in Washington, DC. Eventually, he found a book with a section on the US Army Signal Corps weather code, and with it, he felt he was onto something.

He discovered the cryptogram was a series of weather observations from May 27, 1888. For example, *Bismark Omit leafage buck bank* translated to a weather report from Bismarck, North Dakota: *Bismark* was the location, *Omit* meant 56°F (13°C), *leafage* indicated a dew point of 32°F (0°C) at 10 p.m., *buck* described clear skies, no precipitation and a north wind, and *bank* signaled a wind speed of 12 miles (19 kilometers) per hour. Chan's discovery was confirmed when he matched the codes to historical weather records.

THE MYSTERY REMAINS

While the code was cracked, questions linger about the dress's owner and why the message was hidden. The dress had a label with the name Bennett, but Chan found no records of a Bennett working at the US Signal Corps at the time. The most likely explanation is that the papers were left in the pocket by someone who worked with weather codes, and the dress was simply stored away, preserving the hidden message for over a century. Chan believes there are still clues out there that will help reveal the identity of the dress's owner.

Wayne Chan cracked the cryptogram hidden in a silk dress, once ranked among the top 50 unsolved ciphers.
SARA RIVERS-COFIELD

1467
Cipher disk
1918
The Enigma
1930s
SIGABA cipher machine
1937
The Purple Machine
2000
Invention of CAPTCHA
captcha

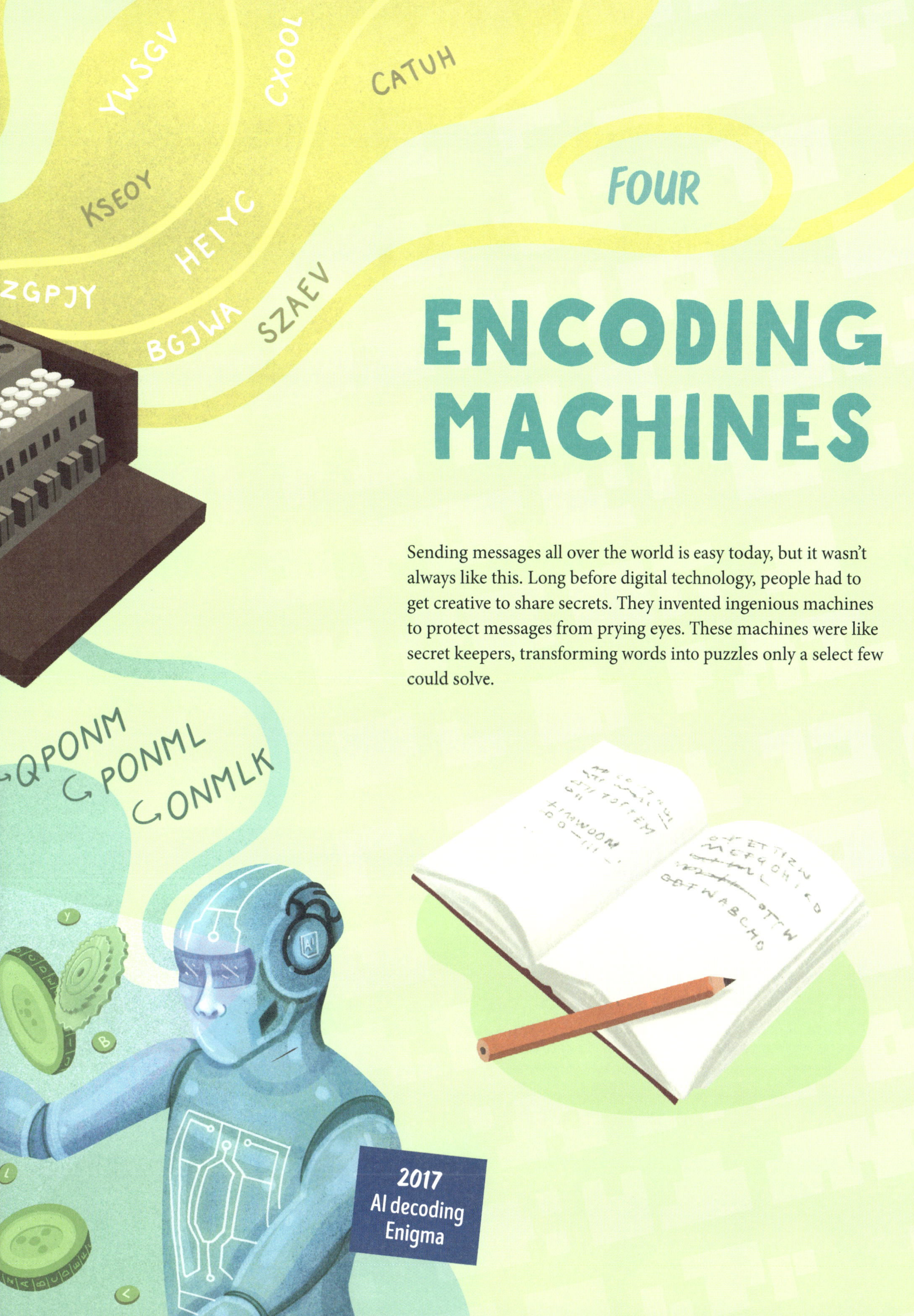

FOUR

ENCODING MACHINES

Sending messages all over the world is easy today, but it wasn't always like this. Long before digital technology, people had to get creative to share secrets. They invented ingenious machines to protect messages from prying eyes. These machines were like secret keepers, transforming words into puzzles only a select few could solve.

Cipher Disk

Leon Battista Alberti

Late 1400s

Italy

During times of war, the cipher disk was a soldier's secret weapon. Small enough to fit in a pocket, it featured two rotating disks, both marked with the alphabet. One disk was used for plaintext, and the other for the corresponding cipher. Soldiers used it to transform commands such as "meet at midnight" into a scrambled string of letters. What was the secret behind these codes? They could only be decoded by someone with a matching disk. At its destination, an officer equipped with the same cipher disk would unravel the code, uncovering the original command. This tool helped keep sensitive military strategies hidden from the enemy.

MECHANIZED SECRETS

The cipher disk is the first mechanical language encryptor. Invented by Leon Battista Alberti, it consisted of two copper disks, each ***engraved*** with the alphabet. The smaller disk sat on the larger one, joined by a pin, allowing each to spin independently. This design made codemaking quicker, easier and less prone to mistakes compared to using complex tables like the Vigenère cipher.

A popular use of cipher disks today is in escape rooms, where players solve puzzles and codes to advance in the game.
HUBERT BERBERICH/WIKIMEDIA COMMONS/PUBLIC DOMAIN

THE ART OF ENCRYPTION

The cipher disk works in two ways. The first uses the Caesar-cipher technique, ***aligning*** the alphabets on the two different disks to shift the letters. For instance, align *A* on the outer disk with *E* on the inner one, and the alphabet shifts four places. Encrypting a message means matching each letter from the outer disk to its counterpart on the inner disk, effectively scrambling the words.

The second method of using the cipher disk adds an extra layer of security by changing the alignment of the disks during the encoding. Encoding is the process of putting a message into a coded form using a specific system or key. Decoding is the process of turning the coded message back into its original form using the same system or key.

For this method, imagine you're encoding the word *HELLO*. You start by setting a shift of three places. Align *A* on the outer disk with *D* on the inner disk. This turns *H* to *K* and *E* to *H*. After encoding two letters, you shift the disks one letter to the right. Now *L* aligns with *P*. Continue on this way, shifting the disks after each two letters you encode.

Shifting the disks intermittently—in this case, after every two letters—makes the code much harder to crack. It continuously changes the encoding pattern, significantly increasing the security of the message.

Alberti's invention was used for centuries and was utilized extensively during the American Civil War. Both the Union and Confederate forces used cipher disks to keep troop movements and battle plans confidential.

Pssst! Many students use creative ways to keep their communications secret, like coded messages or folded notes in fun origami shapes.
LWA/DANN TARDIF/GETTY IMAGES

LILGRAPHER/SHUTTERSTOCK.COM

Securing the Digital World

Drawing inspiration from traditional ciphers like the Caesar cipher, the CAPTCHA in 2000 and reCAPTCHA in 2007 brought a modern twist to internet security, which you've likely seen online. All of these puzzles are easily solvable by humans but challenging for machines. For example, reCAPTCHA may ask you to identify all the images with stop signs, which is simple for people but difficult for automated machines or bots. Using images to filter out bots is similar to the Caesar cipher's technique of shifting the letters to encode messages. Similarly, CAPTCHA scrambles text in a way that filters out automated access, ensuring only humans can access websites.

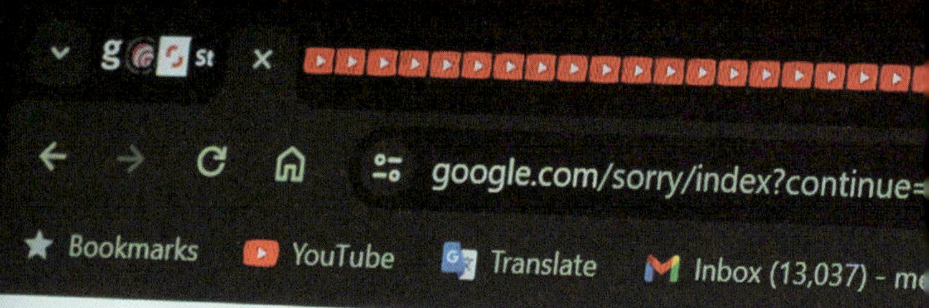

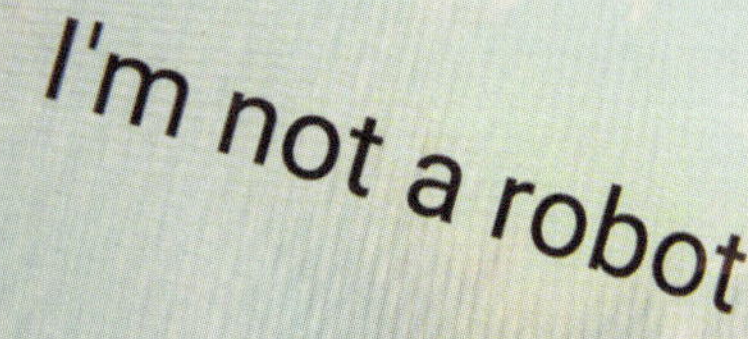

GEORGEJMCLITTLE/DREAMSTIME.COM

ROKAS TENYS/SHUTTERSTOCK.COM

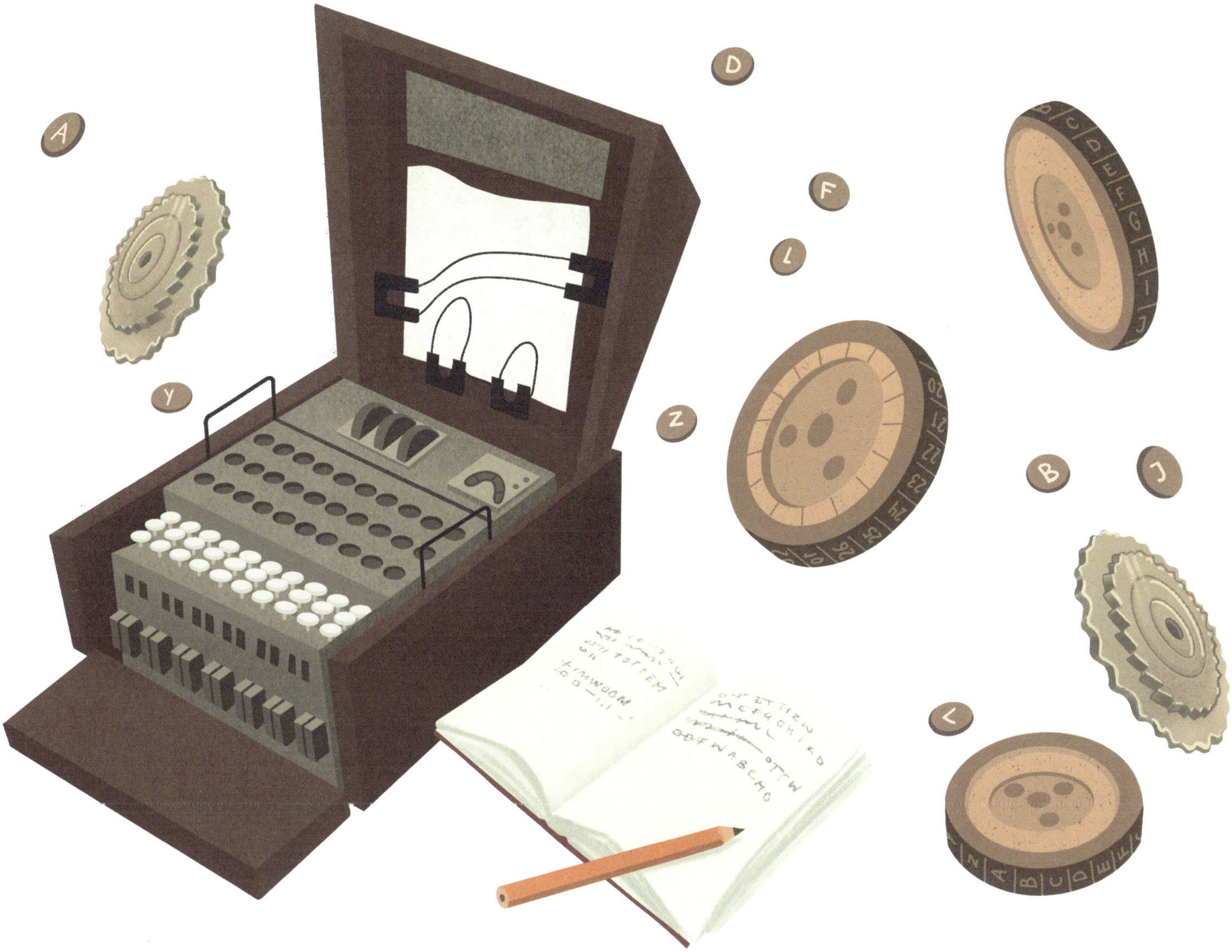

The Enigma

After World War I, governments around the world increased their efforts to create unbreakable codes. Elizebeth Smith Friedman, a renowned American codebreaker who worked during both world wars, remembers that "all the countries of the world were trying to develop something that nobody else could read. They were all playing with machines." Among these inventions, one stood out—the Enigma. Invented by German engineer Arthur Scherbius in 1918, the Engima was the ultimate encryption engine. It gave the Germans an edge during World War II, and for a time they had the most secure communications in the world.

Breaking codes isn't easy, but with the right tools, even the toughest patterns can be cracked.
EMMA FARRER/GETTY IMAGES

ENIGMA'S INNER WORKINGS

The Enigma machine had a unique design. Think of a typewriter that instead of typing letters scrambles them into codes. At the Enigma's core were three spinning wheels, called rotors. Each wheel had an alphabet of its own. Typing a letter, such as *A*, would turn it into a different letter, such as *N*. This letter then passed through the second and and third wheels, which each changed the letter again. Each press of a key would cause the wheels to turn, changing the letter encoding with every keystroke. The result? The same letter could be encoded in multiple ways. There was no pattern, and the selection of letters was completely random.

The machine's settings were changed daily, with different starting positions for the wheels and various connections in its plugboard—a panel with jacks for plugging in cables. With these ***adjustable*** settings, the Enigma could produce billions of possible combinations. To decode the message, the person at the other end needed another Enigma machine set up exactly the same way. If everything matched, the message would appear in plaintext.

Germany adopted the Enigma in 1930, and it became an important tool in their military communications. Military officials sent orders, planned attacks and shared vital information, secure in their belief that the Enigma codes were unbreakable.

THE FALL OF THE ENIGMA

But they shouldn't have been so confident. Allied codebreakers who intercepted the encrypted messages suspected that a complex machine was behind them. They worked nonstop to figure out the Enigma code. Cracking it was a huge moment, giving the Allies important information that helped turn the tide of the war in their favor. Unbeknownst to the Germans, their once-thought-to-be-unbreakable Enigma code had been cracked, leaving their strategies exposed to their enemies.

Purple
Japan's Cipher Machine

Japan protected its secret messages during World War II with a complex cipher machine called Purple, which was similar to the Enigma. Unlike the Enigma, however, Purple used a system based on old telephone switchboards, using plugs and switches to scramble messages. Its settings could be changed daily. But American codebreakers, under William Friedman's leadership, managed to break the Purple code without ever laying eyes on the machine. By studying intercepted messages, they built their own Purple, unlocking Japan's secret communications.

MARK PELLEGRINI/WIKIMEDIA COMMONS/CC BY-SA 2.5

SIGABA

William Friedman and Frank Rowlett

1935

United States

During World War II, the United States had a top-secret weapon in the war of codes—the SIGABA cipher machine. Invented by William Friedman and Frank Rowlett, SIGABA was a cipher machine like no other. Picture a machine with 15 rotating wheels—far more than the Enigma's three or four. Each one scrambled messages in a special way. But SIGABA did something extra clever. It didn't just turn its wheels like other machines. Instead, some wheels controlled how other wheels moved.

SIGABA was so secure that even after World War II, the machine remained classified. Its advanced encryption methods were kept secret until the 1990s, long after newer technology had emerged.
WIKIMEDIA COMMONS/PUBLIC DOMAIN

SIGABA was considered far more secure than Germany's Enigma machine and was never cracked during the war. It was the only encryption system used in World War II that remained completely unbroken.
STEVEN FINE

CLEVER COGS AND WHEELS

The 15 wheels were divided into three separate groups. The first set, the cipher rotors, did the main job of mixing up the letters. The second set, the control rotors, decided how the first set should move. And the third set, the index rotors, helped in this complicated process but didn't move during the encoding. The action of these wheels turned ordinary messages into impenetrable codes. Even if someone knew what the original message was, figuring out how SIGABA scrambled it was almost impossible. It was like solving a puzzle when the pieces constantly changed shape.

But SIGABA's complexity came at a cost. The machine was bulky, heavy and not as easy to transport as the German Enigma. So while it was great for important messages sent from secure locations, it wasn't handy for soldiers on the move. That's why other, simpler machines were often used in the field. SIGABA was among the last of the great mechanical cipher machines built before the world shifted to using computers for encryption.

Solving puzzles isn't just fun—it's a great workout for your brain! Studies show that doing puzzles can improve memory, boost problem-solving skills and even increase IQ by a few points!
HESHPHOTO/GETTY IMAGES

With advances in AI, machines are learning to solve complex puzzles and spot patterns, and they might soon take on challenges once thought impossible.
GORODENKOFF/GETTY IMAGES

Artificial Intelligence (AI) versus Enigma

Modern cryptographers and AI researchers

2017

Imperial War Museum, London, England

Using a blend of old and new technologies, AI researchers conducted an experiment to see how quickly ***artificial intelligence*** could crack the Enigma cipher. They fed AI systems the same coded messages that confused the Allies during World War II. AI used advanced calculations and pattern-spotting techniques similar to the ones used by human codebreakers at Bletchley Park.

BREAKING RECORDS

Surprisingly, the AI systems decoded the Enigma codes in just 13 minutes, with around 41 million combinations tested per second. This success not only highlighted major advancements in computing power and algorithm design but also showed how AI can solve old codes and improve cybersecurity today.

1913
Riverbank
Laboratories
1939
Bletchley Park
1941
Camp X
X
TODAY
National Security
Agency Headquarters

FIVE

SECRET CIPHER SCHOOLS

In a world where decoding secrets could determine whether a country would win a war and could reveal who its friends and enemies were and how it traded with other countries, cipher schools emerged, training the sharpest minds in the art of codebreaking. At these clandestine academies, which operated in the shadows, brilliant minds learned to unravel complex ciphers. The training these schools provided played a crucial role in shaping the art of codebreaking on a global scale, proving that knowledge can be just as mighty as any weapon.

Riverbank Laboratories

George Fabyan

1913–1918

Geneva, Illinois

An alligator pool, a bear cage, a Japanese garden, two windmills, a lighthouse and greenhouses full of flowers—all this and more existed at Riverbank, a 350-acre (1.4-square-kilometer) estate in Geneva, Illinois. It was owned by George Fabyan, a millionaire businessman with a flair for the unusual. But behind all this luxury lay something extraordinary.

Fabyan's estate housed Riverbank Laboratories, a ***think tank*** where scientists studied everything from plant genetics to physical fitness. Fabyan was driven by a passion for solving mysteries and discovering new things. This motivation led him to form a team of codebreakers in 1916. Their first task? Unraveling the secret ciphers Fabyan believed were hidden in Shakespeare's plays.

THE BIRTH OF AMERICAN CODEBREAKING

But the focus at Riverbank Laboratories changed when the United States entered World War I. In 1917, following the interception of the Zimmermann telegram, the government realized it needed people who were skilled in decoding enemy messages. But there was a problem. The United States didn't have any people with experience in breaking codes, and codebreaking agencies didn't exist yet. Seizing the opportunity, Fabyan established the country's first codebreaking team, the Riverbank Department of Ciphers. It was led by two top codebreakers, Elizebeth and William Friedman.

For eight months, secret enemy communications intercepted from Germany and Mexico were brought to Riverbank for decoding. The Friedmans and their team tirelessly cracked streams of codes, turning gibberish into valuable information. To do this, they used statistics, counted the frequency of letters and discovered patterns in ways never seen before in ***cryptanalysis***. Together they developed a series of techniques that laid the foundation for modern cryptology and paved the way for the future National Security Agency (NSA).

Working on a challenge! This student deciphers a tricky puzzle on the whiteboard, mastering skills like those used by wartime codebreakers. Each clue takes them another step closer to unlocking the secret message.
NATALIA BODROVA/GETTY IMAGES

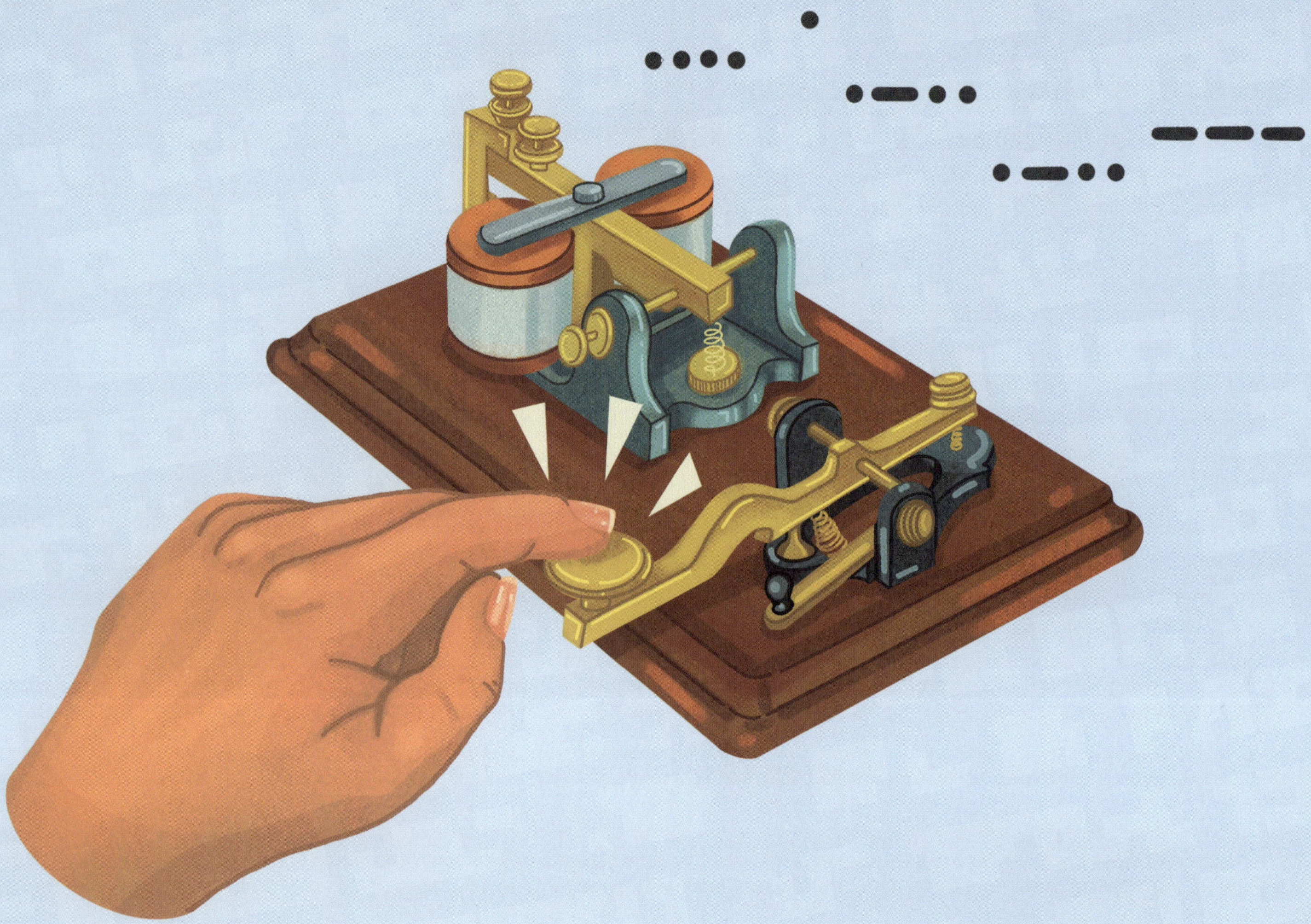

Morse Code

Before radio, messages in battles were carried by horseback or sent through the post office. With the invention of radio, communication changed dramatically. Now messages could be sent through the airwaves in Morse code, a system of tones and clicks representing letters. However, these radio messages could be intercepted by anyone listening in. To protect their secrets, the military began encrypting messages before broadcasting them. This shift to wireless communication meant that more skilled codebreakers needed to be trained, as decoding messages was critical to military strategizing.

A	• ▬
B	▬ • • •
C	▬ • ▬ •
D	▬ • •
E	•
F	• • ▬ •
G	▬ ▬ •
H	• • • •
I	• •
J	• ▬ ▬ ▬
K	▬ • ▬
L	• ▬ • •
M	▬ ▬
N	▬ •
O	▬ ▬ ▬
P	• ▬ ▬ •
Q	▬ ▬ • ▬
R	• ▬ •
S	• • •
T	▬
U	• • ▬
V	• • • ▬
W	• ▬ ▬
X	▬ • • ▬
Y	▬ • ▬ ▬
Z	▬ ▬ • •
1	• ▬ ▬ ▬ ▬
2	• • ▬ ▬ ▬
3	• • • ▬ ▬
4	• • • • ▬
5	• • • • •
6	▬ • • • •
7	▬ ▬ • • •
8	▬ ▬ ▬ • •
9	▬ ▬ ▬ ▬ •
0	▬ ▬ ▬ ▬ ▬

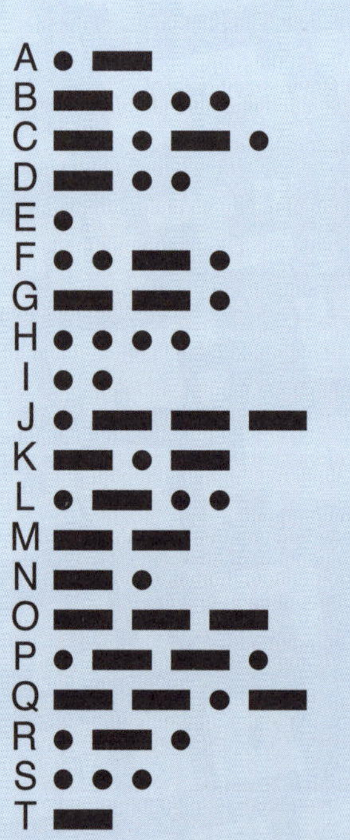

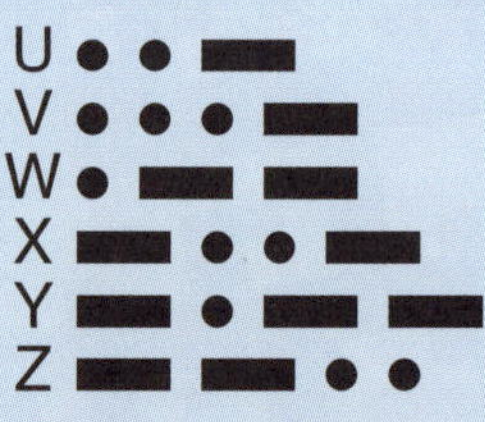

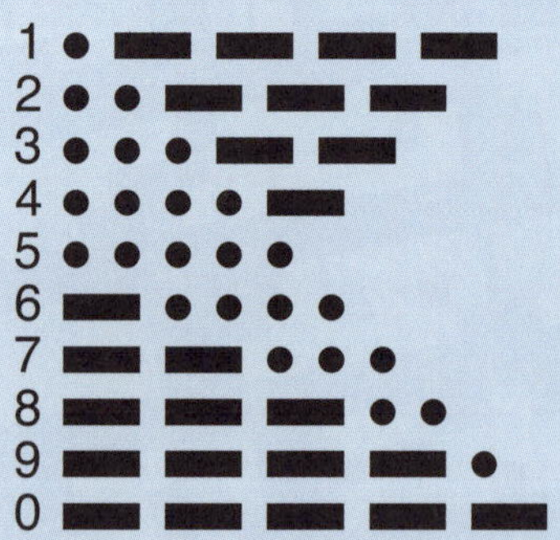

Bletchley Park

Bletchley Park, once a quiet estate, became the center of codebreaking during World War II. Over 9,000 people worked here in secret, helping to crack enemy codes and changing the course of history.

Codebreakers

1939–1945

Milton Keynes, Buckinghamshire, England

Nestled in the English town of Milton Keynes, Buckinghamshire, sits Bletchley Park. During World War II, this once-quiet country house was transformed into a hive of secret activity known as the ***Government Code and Cypher School***. It was here that some of the smartest people came together with one crucial mission: to intercept and decode enemy communications.

CRACKING THE UNBREAKABLE CODES

The task of breaking the codes from the German Enigma and another machine called the Lorenz, both sophisticated cipher devices, was daunting. However, under the leadership of famous codebreaker Alan Turing, a dedicated team developed the Bombe machine. This innovative device sifted through endless possibilities, searching for the key to Enigma's complex encryption. At last it found the right settings, revealing the secrets hidden in Enigma's messages. This breakthrough allowed access to Germany's secret war plans and strategies. Alongside the Bombe, another important development was the Colossus, the world's first programmable digital computer.

The intelligence work done at Bletchley Park was code-named Ultra. It was later revealed by British intelligence that the information gained from the Bombe machine shortened World War II by two to four years, saving countless lives.

Enigma's dials, or rotors, were the heart of its encryption system. Each rotor shifted letters as they passed through, scrambling the message. The operator could adjust the dials to different settings, creating millions of possible combinations. The Bombe machine was developed to crack Enigma's complex encryption.

GCHQ's high-security building, known as the "doughnut," is located in Cheltenham, England. Protected by razor wire, security checkpoints and cameras, this facility helps defend the UK against thousands of weekly cyberattacks.
ADRIAN PINGSTONE/WIKIMEDIA COMMONS/PUBLIC DOMAIN

BLETCHLEY'S LEGACY

In 1946, after World War II ended, the codebreaking activities at Bletchley Park stopped, and the amazing work done there remained a secret until the mid-1970s. The British government kept it under wraps to ensure that its advanced codebreaking techniques didn't fall into the wrong hands.

Bletchley's legacy goes beyond its wartime contributions. It's known as the starting point for today's Government Communications Headquarters (GCHQ), the UK's intelligence, security and cyber organization. The techniques and methods developed at Bletchley laid the groundwork for modern cryptographic practices and ***intelligence gathering.***

Today Bletchley Park is a museum and historical landmark. It's a place where people can explore the secret history of codes and ciphers and learn about the work that shaped the outcome of World War II and the future of secret communications.

Germany's Codebreakers

Germany had its own codebreaking team in World War II, called B-Dienst (short for Beobachtungsdienst, or observation service). Based in Berlin, this team's expert codebreakers were tasked with deciphering the Allies' secret messages. They listened to radio signals, trying to interpret the codes of the countries fighting against Germany. Their work was crucial for the German navy, giving them insights into enemy plans such as upcoming attacks on their submarines or troop movements. But in late 1943, a massive air raid on Berlin hit B-Dienst hard. It destroyed important records and weakened the team's codebreaking abilities.

GEORGE TRUMPETER/SHUTTERSTOCK.COM

Colossus

In the secret rooms of Bletchley Park in 1943, Alan Turing and his team engineered a marvel—the Colossus. Unlike other codecracking machines, the Colossus could be programmed to follow specific instructions, which means it could be set up to perform tasks or solve problems based on the needs of the codebreakers. This flexibility made it an important step toward the digital technology we use today.

To protect its secrets, the Colossus was destroyed after the war. The experts who worked on it at Bletchley Park were sworn to silence, and the blueprints for the machine were also destroyed. The world's first computer vanished without a trace. This allowed other people to take credit for the invention of the first computer.

THE NATIONAL ARCHIVES (UNITED KINGDOM)/WIKIMEDIA COMMONS/PUBLIC DOMAIN

STEVE SIMMONS/DREAMSTIME.COM

Colossus weighed over 2,000 pounds and filled an entire room with 1,500 vacuum tubes powering its codebreaking abilities. Its existence remained a secret for 32 years, with details only becoming public in 1975.

Canada's Camp X

Sir William Stephenson

1941

Near Whitby, Ontario

In the 1940s, a training school and radio communications center operated on the shores of Lake Ontario. It was called Camp X, and it wasn't your typical school—it was a top-secret spy camp. The location was chosen for its seclusion and natural barriers. Surrounded by forests, swamps and rocky hillsides, Camp X was the perfect setting for undercover training. It was also an ideal spot for bouncing radio signals between Europe and the United States, making it easy to coordinate intelligence efforts. Five hundred spies from Canada, the United States and other allied countries honed their skills at Camp X, preparing for critical missions overseas.

Camp X went by several names. The Canadian military nicknamed it Project-J. The Royal Canadian Mounted Police called it S25-1-1. And the British Special Operations Executive, a branch of MI6, called it STS-103 (Special Training School 103).

THE NEED FOR SPIES

World War II started on September 3, 1939, when Germany's invasion of Poland led Britain and France to declare war on Germany, led by Adolf Hitler. Canada followed suit on September 10. By 1940, German forces had conquered much of Europe, and many people feared they would continue to advance. The British prime minister, Winston Churchill, decided to conduct a secret war. He would send undercover spies behind enemy lines to disrupt German operations from the inside. But first those spies needed proper training.

THE BIRTH OF CAMP X

Camp X officially opened on December 6, 1941. Churchill put famous spymaster William Stephenson, from Winnipeg, Manitoba, in charge of running the school. Students would learn how to parachute, disguise themselves and dodge bullets, but this was just the beginning. Trainees were taught silent killing techniques, sabotage and demolition. They also mastered map reading, weaponry and Morse code. While at Camp X, security rules were strict—first names only and no sharing the details of their upcoming mission. Those who did well at Camp X moved on to more advanced academies in Europe.

At Camp X, workers diligently transcribed incoming messages, a vital part of World War II intelligence operations. The smaller photo shows Hydra's main transmitter, which played a key role, securely sending and receiving secret messages over vast distances.

WHITBY PUBLIC LIBRARY ARCHIVE/PUBLIC DOMAIN

LYNN PHILIP HODGSON/CAMP-X.COM

HYDRA

In addition to the training grounds of Camp X was an advanced radio system made up of towering antennae, powerful transmitters and receivers for sending and receiving signals. It was called Hydra, and with it, agents in North America and the United Kingdom could exchange vital encoded information in a matter of seconds.

At the core of Camp X was its communications building, a bustling hub of activity. Within these walls skilled men and women diligently worked to transcribe, decode and re-encode the encrypted messages flowing through Hydra. They ensured that vital information was exchanged, decoded and sent to where it was needed most.

END OF AN ERA

By 1944 Camp X had served its purpose, and its doors were closed. Its records were either secured or destroyed, and in 1969 the site was decommissioned. All but one of the buildings were demolished in the late 1970s. Today the area is known as Intrepid Park, with a monument honoring the bravery of those who trained and worked at Camp X.

The National Security Agency (NSA)

Established by
Harry S. Truman

1952

Fort Meade, Maryland

On November 4, 1952, then US president Harry S. Truman made an important decision. He established the National Security Agency (NSA) to protect the American people. Truman saw the need for a dedicated team to keep the United States safe by intercepting and decoding secret messages from other nations. This new agency built on the successful codebreaking work of Elizebeth and William Friedman during World Wars I and II. The agency was kept a secret until 1975, when it was revealed to the public.

GOD4ATHER/SHUTTERSTOCK.COM

The NSA was nicknamed No Such Agency because of its extreme secrecy. For years the agency's existence wasn't publicly acknowledged, fueling mystery and curiosity about its operations. Despite its public role today, much of its work remains highly classified.
NATIONAL SECURITY AGENCY/WIKIMEDIA COMMONS/PUBLIC DOMAIN

SIGINT can collect signals from things like phones, radios and even satellites! These signals help experts decode secret messages and spot hidden threats.
ALEX SHOLOM/GETTY IMAGES

GUARDIANS OF SECRETS

The NSA's mission is to protect American citizens by listening to conversations all over the world. This global eavesdropping is called signals intelligence, or SIGINT. By gathering, decoding and examining information, the NSA uncovers hidden threats, keeping the country safe from spies and terrorists. It also works to keep other countries from listening in on the United States. Secret methods used include planting listening devices in electronic systems and sending out computer viruses to stop enemies from stealing information.

SECRECY AND CHANGE

After the terrorist attacks on September 11, 2001, when almost 3,000 people were killed in the United States, the NSA's role grew to include monitoring terrorist threats from inside the country without prior approval from special courts. This has led to debates about privacy and the balance between individual freedoms and national security. Some people worry that these measures might trespass on citizens' privacy rights, while others believe they are necessary to prevent future attacks and keep the country safe.

In 2013 former NSA intelligence contractor Edward Snowden leaked information about the NSA's surveillance programs, which are designed to watch and collect information from communications between people. Again, this sparked discussions worldwide about citizens' need for privacy and the government's need for surveillance.

LOOKING AHEAD

Today the NSA continues to use advanced technology to keep the nation safe, while being monitored to ensure it respects people's privacy. It focuses on stopping cyberattacks, monitoring potential threats and protecting government communications. Whether guarding against cyberthreats or deciphering coded information, the NSA plays an important role in national security.

The word *eavesdropping* comes from medieval times, when people would hide under the eaves of a building's roof to secretly listen in on conversations inside.
FRANZ12/GETTY IMAGES

1892
Elizebeth Smith Friedman

1912
Alan Turing

1918
Charles "Checker" Tomkins

1935
Elsa Lessard and the Wrens

CODING HEROES

1917
Joan Clarke

Cryptographers often work out of the spotlight, turning complicated puzzles into valuable information. Their skills in decoding have influenced not just battles but also business, trade, politics and peace negotiations, showing that sometimes the most powerful tool in any conflict is the ability to solve a mystery.

2018
Avye Couloute

Elizebeth Smith Friedman

Pioneer Cryptologist

1892–1980

United States

Elizebeth Smith Friedman wasn't a mathematician or a scientist. She was a poet who had a gift for seeing the patterns contained in words. Throughout her career, Elizebeth cracked hundreds of codes, helped establish the United States Department of War's first cryptology division and played an important role in both world wars. She began her remarkable career at Riverbank Laboratories, one of the spy schools mentioned in chapter 5. It's where she met her future husband and partner in codebreaking, William Friedman.

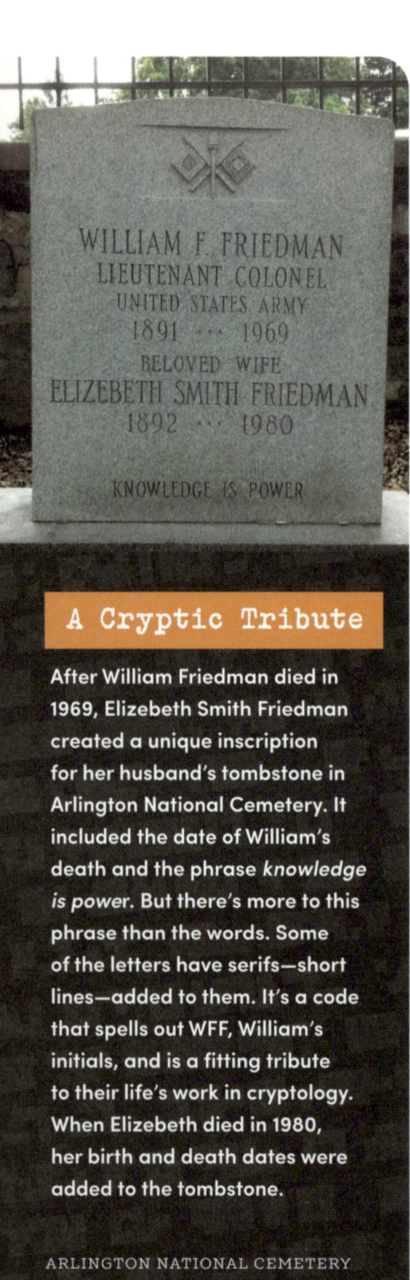

A Cryptic Tribute

After William Friedman died in 1969, Elizebeth Smith Friedman created a unique inscription for her husband's tombstone in Arlington National Cemetery. It included the date of William's death and the phrase *knowledge is power*. But there's more to this phrase than the words. Some of the letters have serifs—short lines—added to them. It's a code that spells out WFF, William's initials, and is a fitting tribute to their life's work in cryptology. When Elizebeth died in 1980, her birth and death dates were added to the tombstone.

ARLINGTON NATIONAL CEMETERY EXPLORER/WIKIMEDIA COMMONS/ PUBLIC DOMAIN

BLAZING A TRAIL

Together the Friedmans made an unbeatable team. When World War I started, they tackled a flurry of secret messages intercepted by the US Navy. Elizebeth wrote in her diary that so little was known of codebreaking at the time that "we ourselves had to be the learners, the workers, and the teachers all at one and the same time." Elizebeth wasn't just breaking codes: she was pioneering a new field by also teaching the military's first codebreakers.

THE PROHIBITION CHALLENGE

In 1925 Elizebeth faced a new challenge—prohibition. The sale of alcohol was banned in the United States at that time and had turned the seas into highways for illegal alcohol smuggling. The Coast Guard was struggling to catch the ***mobsters*** who concealed their smuggling routes using encrypted radio messages. They needed someone who had the skills to break these codes. Elizebeth was the perfect choice. She cracked two years' worth of the smugglers' secret messages in just three months, disrupting their plans and stopping shipments of alcohol. Elizebeth became a key witness in several big trials that helped convict some of the world's toughest criminals, including gangster Al Capone.

A HEROINE OF WORLD WAR II

The stakes were even higher in World War II. A spy ring was leaking Allied ship locations to German U-boats (submarines) using coded messages. More than 5,000 seamen had lost their lives in the U-boat attacks. Elizebeth was tasked with breaking those codes. Her breakthrough came when she deciphered plans targeting the RMS *Queen Mary*, carrying 8,398 American servicemen. Her discovery allowed the captain of the ship to sneak past German submarines, saving the lives of the entire crew.

At the same time, as we've already learned, codebreakers around the world were racing to decode Enigma's secrets. Friedman's chance came when an Enigma operator carelessly failed to change the machine's settings between messages. It took months, but Elizebeth and her team broke three separate Enigma machines.

Because of the highly confidential nature of their work, Elizebeth was unaware that other codebreakers like Alan Turing had also decrypted Enigma around the same time. By December 1942, her team had broken all of the Nazis' new codes, decrypted over 4,000 messages from enemy spies and dismantled every underground spy network in South America.

UNSUNG HERO

Elizebeth's wartime efforts were a closely guarded secret. She took an oath of silence, watching as others, like FBI director J. Edgar Hoover, got credit for her work. It wasn't until 2008, years after she had died, that her incredible contributions in locating Nazis in South America during World War II were fully acknowledged, marking her as one of history's great codebreakers.

Alan Mathison Turing

Mathematician and Logician

June 23, 1912–June 7, 1954

Born in London, England

Alan Turing's work at Bletchley Park built upon the efforts of Polish codebreaker Marian Rejewski and his team. After the Polish team shared the blueprints and a model of the Enigma that they had built, Turing took on the challenge of adapting and developing these initial breakthroughs. Amid the constant hum of machines, he was on a critical mission to unravel the Enigma code, a sophisticated puzzle whose settings the Nazis changed regularly to protect their secrets. As we read in chapter 5, Turing's answer to this complex challenge was the creation of the Bombe.

Day after day, Turing observed Bombe's rows of spinning rotors and tangled network of wires. His mind relentlessly tackled a complicated maze of challenges, such as matching up the machine's rotors to match the Enigma's settings or improving its mechanical pieces to prevent jams. Turing worked tirelessly to improve the machine. Each attempt, setback and tweak brought him a step closer to the solution he needed.

A PRODIGY IN MATHEMATICS

Born in London in 1912, Turing showed a remarkable talent for numbers from a young age. He was fascinated by mathematics and logic. Turing flourished when he got to King's College, Cambridge, and earned a first-class honors degree in mathematics.

Turing joined Bletchley Park's Government Code and Cypher School in 1939. He worked with a team of codebreakers, including renowned codebreaker Gordon Welchman, to build the Bombe. In March 1940 their hard work paid off. The Bombe successfully broke through the Enigma code, unlocking important German military secrets, including the locations of their submarines. By early 1942 the team at Bletchley was decoding a staggering 39,000 messages a month. This gave Britain a much-needed edge, and by 1945 the Allies had won the war. Turing's pivotal role earned him recognition as an Officer of the Most Excellent Order of the British Empire.

A LIFE CUT SHORT

Despite his monumental achievements, Turing's personal life took a harsh turn in 1952. He was convicted for having a relationship with a man, an illegal act in the United Kingdom at the time. This conviction led to the loss of his job and ended his work with the government's codebreaking center. Turing spent his final years at Manchester University, researching how to create artificial life, until he died in 1954 at the age of 42 under mysterious circumstances. In a long-overdue act of justice, the law against homosexuality was abolished in the UK in 1967, and Turing received a royal pardon in 2013.

In honor of his contributions to computer science, the A.M. Turing Award was established in 1966. Often described as "the Nobel Prize of computing," it is awarded every year to individuals who have made significant achievements in the field, including Canadian Yoshua Bengio and British Canadian Geoffrey Hinton. They won the award in 2018 for their work in artificial intelligence.

VERTIGO3D/GETTY IMAGES

The Turing Machines

In 1936 at Princeton University, where Alan Turing completed a doctoral thesis before returning to Cambridge, he sketched the blueprint for the first electronic computer, dubbing it the "a-machine" or "Turing machine." Though the computer was never actually built, the blueprint laid out how a computer could interpret and carry out a set of instructions. Turing's theory formed the foundation of modern computing.

Later, in 1950, Turing wrote an important paper called "Computing Machinery and Intelligence," which explored the question of whether computers could think like humans. He came up with a way to test a computer's intelligence, calling it the "imitation game." Today we know it as the Turing test. If a person interacting with the machine can't easily tell whether they are talking to a human or a machine, the machine is considered to have human-like intelligence. This test was significant in the world of computer science and helped scientists understand more about artificial intelligence.

Joan Clarke

Codebreaker

1917–1996

Dulwich, England

While Elizebeth Smith Friedman blazed trails in North America, another pioneering woman was making her mark in the United Kingdom. Joan Clarke was the only woman on the team in that country that cracked the Enigma during World War II. Like Friedman, Clarke was a leader in a world filled with men.

A MATH WIZARD

In 1936, at Dulwich High School in South London, Clarke's exceptional math skills earned her a scholarship to Newnham College, Cambridge. She graduated with top honors in mathematics. Gordon Welchman, a fellow mathematician, noticed Clarke's talent and invited her to join him at Bletchley Park in 1944. At first she was assigned to clerical tasks and labeled a secretary, but she was soon transferred to Alan Turing's codebreaking team.

MASTERING ENIGMA

At Bletchley, Clarke's skill in recognizing patterns in encrypted messages was crucial. Working closely with Alan Turing and other codebreakers, she quickly became one of the team's best, often staying late to improve her techniques. She and Turing developed a close friendship during their time at Bletchley, working together to crack the codes that were crucial to the Allied war effort.

HER LEGACY

Clarke didn't just break codes. She shattered the barriers for women in her field by excelling as a codebreaker, a job typically held by men at the time. At Bletchley Park, she also became the deputy head of a section called Hut 8. Her achievements paved the way for future generations of women in science and technology.

The Enigma machine had over 150 quintillion possible settings! That's more combinations than there are stars in the Milky Way, making it one of the hardest codes to crack during World War II.

GIOREZ/GETTY IMAGES

Charles "Checker" Tomkins

Cree Code Talker

1918–2003

Born in Grouard, Alberta

Charles "Checker" Tomkins was a Métis man born in Grouard, Alberta, in 1918. He grew up immersed in the Cree language, thanks to his grandparents. Tomkins joined the army in 1940, and after six months of training, he was sent to Britain for a top-secret operation. He was one of about 600 Indigenous soldiers tested for their language skills. Tomkins stood out for his aptitude in Cree.

CREE CODE TALKERS

He and a group of other Métis and Cree soldiers became heroes in the Canadian military as code talkers. They played an important role in war communications, sending secret military messages in Cree, which was mostly unknown outside Cree and Métis communities. When Tomkins and other Cree speakers transmitted messages in Cree via radio, their messages couldn't be deciphered by German forces who might be eavesdropping. This method of relaying messages was faster than any machine, providing a significant advantage to Canadian forces.

ADAPTING LANGUAGE FOR WAR

There was just one problem for the Cree code talkers—their language didn't have words for military equipment. So Tomkins and his fellow Cree speakers developed new terms. They called a Mosquito bomber sakimes (mosquito), a Spitfire plane iskotew (fire) and a Mustang aircraft pakwatastim (wild horse).

Despite the contributions he made during the war, Tomkins faced racism and limited support when he left the military. For a long time, the contributions of Tomkins and his fellow Cree code talkers were kept secret, even from their own families. Only at the age of 85 did Tomkins finally share his story. At the time, he was one of the last living Cree code talkers, and today, he is one of the most well known.

Choctaw Telephone Squad

The Cree code talkers weren't the only people who used their language to confuse the enemy. The Choctaw Telephone Squad was formed during World War I. The squad consisted of 19 Choctaw soldiers, mostly from Oklahoma. Other Native American soldiers also used their language as an unbreakable code. In World War II, Comanche and Navajo code talkers were credited with saving thousands of lives. The Navajo code talkers helped the Allies win several key battles in the Pacific.

The WRENS

Women's Royal Canadian Naval Service (WRCNS)

1942-1946

HMCS Coverdale, New Brunswick

By 1944 more than 74,000 women were serving in the Women's Royal Naval Service (WRNS), in over 200 different roles. Nearly 7,000 women were in the Women's Canadian Royal Naval Service, also called Wrens.

UK GOVERNMENT/WIKIMEDIA COMMONS/PUBLIC DOMAIN

As World War II raged, a group of young women straight out of high school joined the Women's Royal Canadian Naval Service. They were called the Wrens.

THE LISTENERS

In 1942 the Wrens were working out of a signals intelligence station in New Brunswick called HMCS Coverdale. The Wrens listened for messages sent by other countries and intercepted coded messages from German U-boats. They tracked the submarines' locations, providing vital information to American and British Navy commanders.

SECRET OPERATIONS

Elsa Lessard, a Wren at Coverdale, remembered long hours spent listening to static, hoping to hear German communications. Once they caught a message, they quickly encoded it and sent it to Bletchley Park in the UK. Lessard believed that listeners like her, working around the world, helped shorten the war. Dorothy Lincoln, another Wren, worked with advanced codebreaking machines like Colossus, helping crack thousands of messages every month. She remembers how sometimes they knew information before even the high command in Germany.

THEIR CONTRIBUTION

For years the Wrens' work was hidden behind the Official Secrets Act. To the outside world, their jobs were clerical, often labeled as "writer" or "secretary." Only recently have their true roles and crucial contributions to the war effort been recognized.

Teen tech makers like Avye Couloute are leading the way in inspiring more girls to explore coding and robotics. With each new creation, they help close the gender gap and show that technology is for everyone.
TARA MOORE/GETTY IMAGES

Avye Couloute

Founder of Girls Into Coding

2018

London, England

Avye Couloute is an award-winning teen tech maker and a passionate advocate of getting more girls into coding. She started attending coding workshops when she was just seven years old, fascinated by how she could use code to make things move or control electronics. However, she quickly noticed a huge problem—very few girls were sharing this journey with her.

Determined to change this, Couloute launched Girls Into Coding when she was 11 years old. This initiative encourages young girls to explore coding and technology, fields in which the majority of workers are typically male. Girls Into Coding creates opportunities for girls to participate in workshops and get hands-on experience building and programming their own robots.

CREATING OPPORTUNITIES

Couloute's workshops are a blend of fun and learning. Girls receive packages containing the parts to build robots designed by Couloute herself. These robots can do amazing things like wave balloons, pick up objects and even respond to voice commands. One robot can move its arms or open its mouth when you speak into its microphone. Another can measure and display temperature changes on a computer screen, showing how coding can bring ideas to life.

GLOBAL IMPACT

When the COVID-19 pandemic hit, Couloute didn't let it stop her. She moved her workshops online, attracting girls not just from the UK but from around thc world, including the United States, Canada, India, Singapore and Denmark. Seeing the excitement on girls' faces when their robots come to life is one of Couloute's favorite moments. It proves they can code and that what they've built really works.

VISION FOR THE FUTURE

Couloute believes in breaking down stereotypes in computer programming. She wants young women to know about the exciting opportunities that coding skills can offer and show that anyone can excel in technology. With her passion and dedication, Couloute hopes to ensure that every girl who wants to has the chance to explore, learn and thrive in the digital world.

1815
Ada Lovelace

1991
Pretty Good Privacy

TODAY
Bruce Schneier

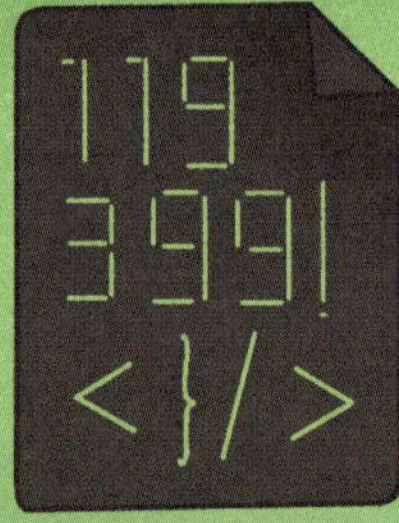

1960s
ASCII—American Standard Code for Information Interchange

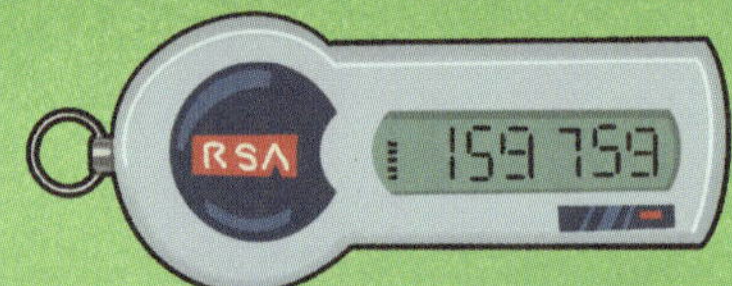

1977
RSA Encryption

TODAY
Canada Revenue Agency scam

SEVEN

CYBERSECURITY

Imagine your online life as a treasure chest filled with secrets. Then think of cybersecurity as the high-tech armor keeping it safe. From your emails and texts to your social media posts, online gaming profiles and YouTube comments, every byte of your digital existence needs protection.

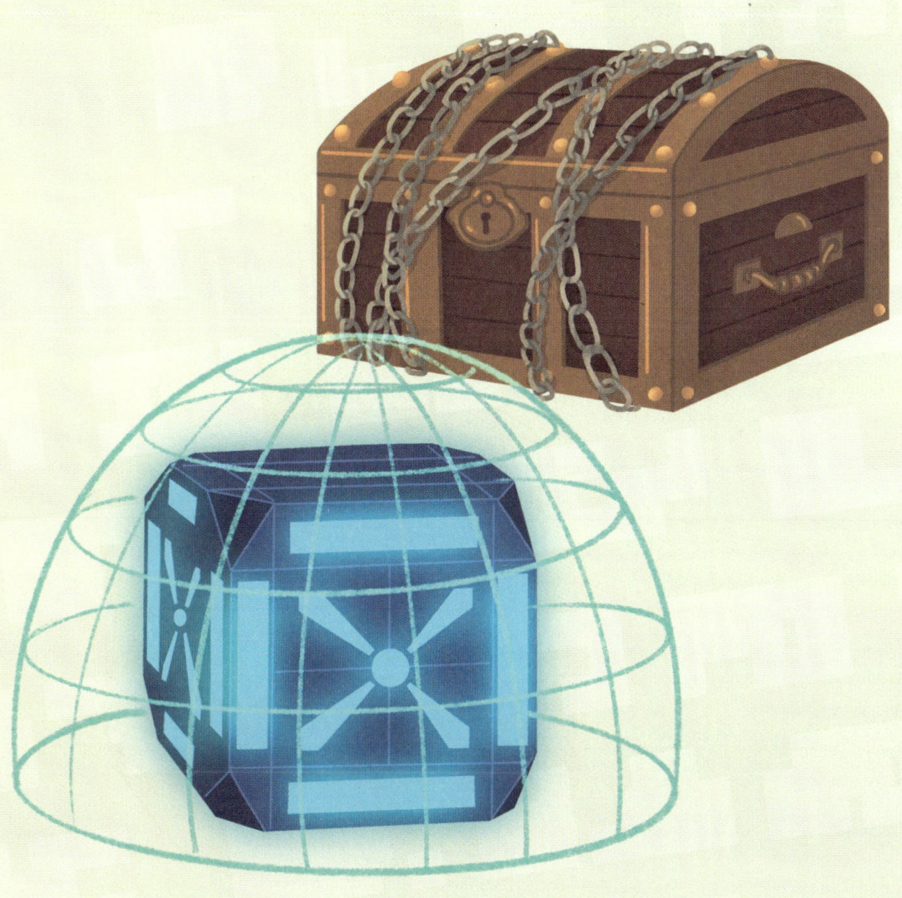

Creating a Computer Language

American Standard Code for Information Interchange (ASCII)

1960s

Washington, DC

When you send an email, it doesn't travel as a collection of regular words. It changes into a special code. Codes that led to the invention of computer programs have been around since the 1800s, long before computers existed. This early work helped shape how computers communicate today.

The first computers were built in the 1930s, starting with Colossus. But they were different than the computers you know. They used plugs and switches to perform tasks. If you wanted them to do a new task, you had to move all the plugs and switches around, rewiring the whole machine each time. But in the 1950s, things changed. Fortran, one of the earliest computer languages, came out in 1957. It gave computers a set of instructions to follow. But each computer still had its own language. This created a problem because computers couldn't easily communicate with each other.

HULTON ARCHIVE/GETTY IMAGES

Ada Lovelace

Born in 1815, Ada Lovelace lived in a world before cars, phones or electricity. Yet she became a trailblazer in computer science. Her work would later inspire World War II codebreaker Alan Turing. Lovelace's fascination with mathematics led her to Charles Babbage, the inventor of an early form of the computer called the Analytical Engine. Lovelace saw something special in this machine, imagining it could create music or art.

Babbage asked Lovelace to translate an article about his calculating machine from French to English. But she did more than just translate. She added her own notes, which were three times longer than the original article. In these notes, she wrote the first-ever computer program. She figured out how the Analytical Engine could calculate a sequence of numbers, showing that a machine could follow a set of instructions, or a program, to solve problems. Although the Analytical Engine was never constructed, its design, along with Lovelace's notes, are considered a model for the first computer.

BINARY: THE COMPUTER'S ABCS

How do computers get things done? They follow programs, which are lists of instructions written by coders. But computers need these instructions translated into ***machine code***, their basic language. Machine code is binary, made up of zeroes and ones. Each zero or one is a way of telling the computer's switches to be on or off. Coders combine these to tell the computer what to do.

THE UNIVERSAL TRANSLATOR

That's where ASCII comes in. It changes our words into binary code, which are the zeros and ones that computers understand. The invention of ASCII in the 1960s was a game changer for computer communication. It assigns numbers to everything. For example, an uppercase *A* is 65, and a lowercase *a* is 97. ASCII covers 128 characters, including letters, numbers and punctuation marks. It even has special instructions for how text looks on the screen. These numbers travel across the internet. When they reach another computer, ASCII turns them back into words. Thanks to ASCII, computers from all over the world can talk to each other.

Future coder at work! Did you know that there are over 700 coding languages in use today—more than twice the number of spoken languages in the United States? Learn a few, like Java or Python, and the rest get easier to pick up.
MEDIAPHOTOS/GETTY IMAGES

RSA Encryption

Ron Rivest, Adi Shamir and Leonard Adleman

1977

Massachusetts Institute of Technology (MIT)

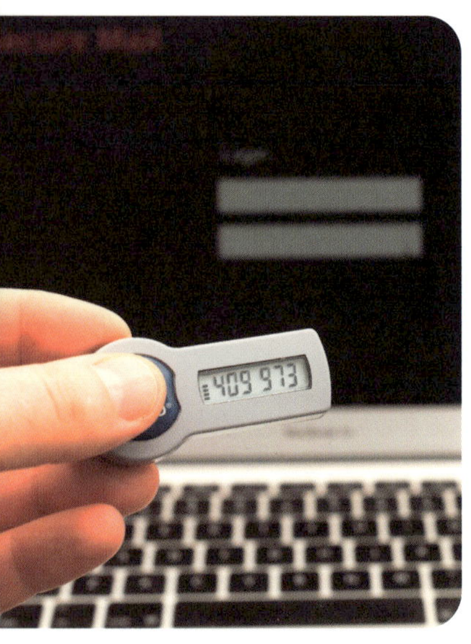

With a secure token in hand, logging in becomes much safer. It generates a unique code every time you log in. This extra step makes sure that even if someone has your password, they still can't get in without the constantly changing code.
AMJONIK.PL/SHUTTERSTOCK.COM

In 1977, just as computers began to connect worldwide, a new problem arose. How would we keep our private information safe in the digital world? ***Hackers***, always looking for a way into computer systems, posed a real threat. And they still do. Hackers are technology experts who know how to bypass security and get into a computer or network. Not all hackers are bad. Some are white-hat hackers, who use their skills to find and fix problems in online systems. On the other hand, black-hat hackers illegally access online systems to steal data or cause harm.

An encryption system known as RSA (the initialism comes from the surnames of creators Ron Rivest, Adi Shamir and Leonard Adleman) was a huge step forward in keeping digital messages secure. It allowed for messages to be sent safely, without giving away access to people's private data.

UNLOCKING RSA'S SECRETS

Imagine RSA encryption is like a treasure chest. Anyone can put things into it, but only you have the special key to open it and see what's inside. So if your friend Ann wants to send you a secret note, she can drop it into the chest using an address that everyone knows, called the public key. But only you have the private key, kind of like a secret code, to unlock the chest and read the note. To anyone else who wants to peek, the chest is locked, and the note inside just looks like a bunch of scribbles and symbols.

VVOE/SHUTTERSTOCK.COM

Who can unlock the right box? Post-office boxes hold important mail, but only the right key can open them. It's just like digital security, where special keys protect your private information from others.
BERND SCHUETTKE/GETTY IMAGES

Today we can shop with just a tap, but behind the scenes, advanced security keeps personal information safe. Every purchase is protected by codes that scramble data, making sure shoppers' details stay private.
DARIOGAONA/GETTY IMAGES

THE POWER OF PRIME NUMBERS

RSA's strength comes from using large prime numbers. Prime numbers are those that can only be divided by 1 and themselves, like 3, 5, 7, 11 and so on. RSA picks two big primes and multiplies them to make a unique key. Cracking RSA encryption means figuring out these prime numbers, which is like looking for a tiny needle in a giant haystack.

RSA remains one of the top choices for encryption worldwide. It played a key role in making online shopping safer by protecting data like credit card information. Today, elliptic curve cryptography (ECC) is also popular. ECC uses the math of ***elliptical curves*** instead of prime numbers. It tends to work faster because it uses smaller keys, but it is just as secure as RSA.

Avoiding Malware Menace

In the digital world, code is powerful but can be misused. ***Malware*** includes things like computer viruses, worms, adware and spyware. Viruses and worms are like sneaky invaders that often hide in emails or downloads. Once you click on them, they spring to life, invading and damaging devices. Adware causes annoying pop-ups, while spyware secretly monitors your activities. To stay safe, avoid suspicious links and use reliable antivirus and anti-malware software.

Pretty Good Privacy (PGP)

Phil Zimmermann

1991

United States

Pretty Good Privacy (PGP) is like a digital lockbox for emails. It's used worldwide for sending private emails without the worry of prying eyes. Just like RSA, it has two special keys to lock and unlock email. Each user has a public key, which is available to everyone, and a private key, which is kept secret. When you send an email, you lock it with the receiver's public key. Only the recipient's private key can unlock it and read the message. To use PGP, individuals need to install the program themselves.

Hidden in Plain Sight

While cryptography is about encoding secret messages to make them unreadable, steganography is about hiding them within something else. It's like digital hide-and-seek—secrets or malware are hidden inside normal-looking images or in audio files. Imagine a spy putting important information, whether it be text, code or a hidden image, in a picture of a mountain or a city street, then posting it online. To us it would just be a picture. But to those in the know, there'd be a secret message inside. It's a clever way to send secrets without drawing attention.

FLAVIO COELHO/GETTY IMAGES

BUILDING TRUST AND SECURITY

PGP is unique in that it lets users confirm each other's keys. They do this through a method called key signing, where users sign each other's keys to verify their identity, a bit like friends vouching for one another. This adds an extra layer of trust, ensuring that the keys belong to the right people. Plus, PGP has a cool trick called hashing. It creates a unique "fingerprint" for each message. When the receiver gets the email, PGP checks to see if the message's fingerprint matches the original one created by the sender. If it does, you know the message is the same as it was when sent, untouched and safe. While PGP is great at keeping emails secure, it's not foolproof. It relies on users keeping their private keys secret and being smart about whom they trust.

Unlock with a touch! Fingerprint authentication uses the unique patterns on your fingers to keep your data secure. No two fingerprints are alike, making this one of the safest ways to protect your information.
DA-KUK/GETTY IMAGES

Security Guru

Bruce Schneier

1963-present

United States

Bruce Schneier always loved solving puzzles. He studied physics and computer science and soon discovered a passion for keeping our digital world safe. Today Schneier's work focuses on encrypting messages so only the intended people can understand and access them. This helps keep our personal information secure.

Email Scams

In a sneaky scam in Canada, fraudsters pretended to be from the Canada Revenue Agency. They sent out fake emails that claimed recipients had a tax refund waiting for them. To get the refund, they were asked to click on a link and enter their personal information, including their social security number and bank details. But there was no refund. The whole thing was a trick to steal people's personal information. The scammers used this information to take money from people's bank accounts and commit ***identity theft***. Always be careful with your personal information, especially in emails that seem too good to be true!

CHAMPIONING A SAFE CYBERSPACE

The 2020 US elections highlighted major cybersecurity issues that could affect any country. Hackers from other countries tried to spread false information, steal data and tamper with ballots to disrupt the voting process. This led to confusion and distrust among voters. The election also showed that online systems aren't as secure as they should be. Schneier argues for stronger cybersecurity to fix weak spots like building better security for voter databases, election software and communication networks. He points out that while countries often spy on each other, combining spying with cyberattacks is a big threat. Cyberattacks can not only steal things like private information, but they can shut down important systems that we rely on every day, like electricity and transportation.

Schneier thinks we need to improve digital defenses, such as firewalls and antivirus programs, and better secure networks to keep our online activity and essential communication channels safe. "Privacy is our right," he says. "It is necessary for maintaining our dignity and respect."

By enhancing security, we can make the internet a safer place for everyone. This means designing systems that involve more than just strong cryptography. He also suggests designing systems that are regularly updated to protect against new threats. It's where "all security measures, including cryptology, work together," he says. Schneier also supports the idea of letting everyone know when there is a problem. Making security issues public can lead to faster fixes and improvements because when people know about problems, they push for solutions. If a hacker broke into the Central Intelligence Agency (CIA), for example, telling people about it could help prevent it from happening again. Good security practices are about more than ensuring that data remains private.

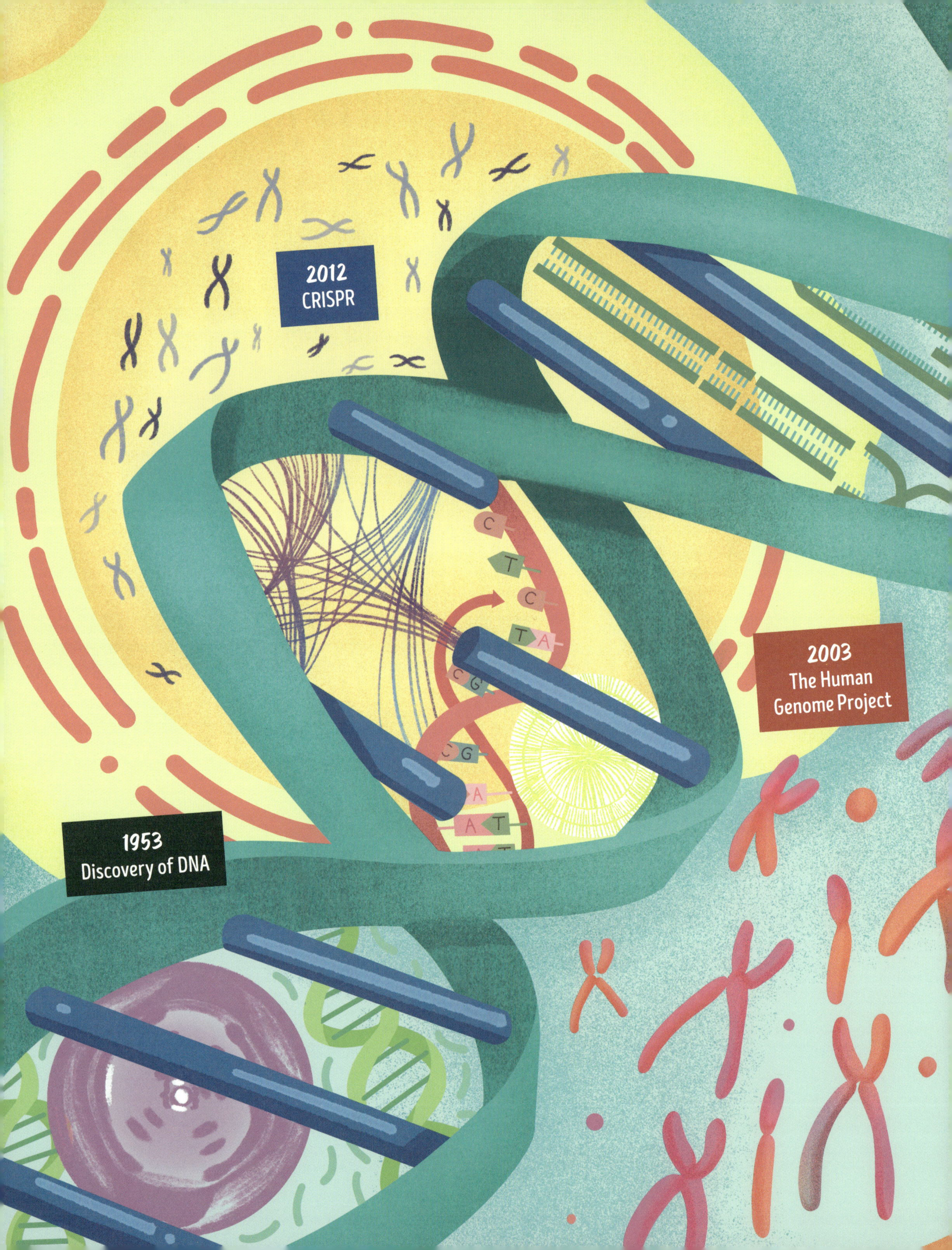
2012
CRISPR
2003
The Human
Genome Project
1953
Discovery of DNA

EIGHT

HACKING THE HUMAN CODE

Picture your body as a book brimming with secrets. Now think of ***genetic*** science as the key that unlocks these mysteries. From eye color to health, every detail of our being is written in a code called DNA.

The Story of DNA

James Watson, Francis Crick, Rosalind Franklin and Maurice Wilkins

1953

Decoding Deoxyribonucleic acid (DNA)

In the 1950s, while mathematicians were busy coding the digital future with ones and zeros, a team of scientists started on an adventure to decode life itself. They uncovered the secrets of DNA, the genetic information for every plant, animal and person.

HOW LIFE IS BUILT

Our bodies are made up of over three billion cells, each with a specific job. Some cells let you see, and others help you run, jump or catch a ball. But how do these cells know what to do? The answer lies in DNA. DNA is like a recipe book inside every cell. But instead of using words, the language of DNA is written with just four letters: *A*, *T*, *G* and *C*. They stand for the nucleotides adenine, thymine, cytosine and guanine. These four compounds mix and match in countless ways. They create a set of instructions that defines everything about you, from the color of your eyes to the way you laugh.

The Pioneers of DNA Discovery

The journey to understand DNA began with Friedrich Miescher, a Swiss chemist who first identified it in 1869. Back then, Miescher knew he had found something significant, but the full importance of DNA was a mystery. Then, in the 1950s, James Watson, Francis Crick, Rosalind Franklin and Maurice Wilkins decoded the entire structure of DNA. Their work, which earned them the Nobel Prize in 1962, transformed our understanding of biology.

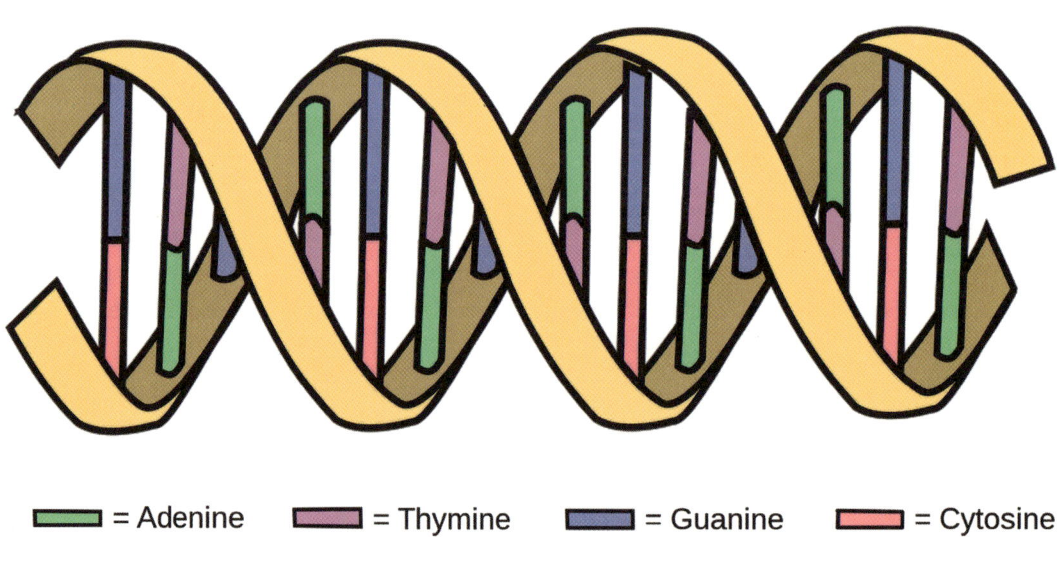

The DNA spiral's "rungs" are held together by a strong phosphate backbone, which gives the structure its twist. This backbone not only supports the DNA but also protects the code inside.
FORLUVOFT/WIKIMEDIA COMMONS/PUBLIC DOMAIN

THE LANGUAGE OF LIFE

Unlike flat letters on a page, DNA forms a shape like a twisting ladder, called a double helix. Imagine a staircase that spirals up. The steps are the DNA compounds, held in place by sides made of atoms and sugars. DNA can split into a single strand, which then makes an exact copy of itself, forming a new double helix.

DNA's words are always three letters long, like ATG or GCA. These are called ***codons***. They join to make a DNA sequence, known as a ***gene***. Each gene tells cells how to make proteins that decide what the cell does.

Genes create life's variety. They make us who we are—whether we have curly or straight hair, blue eyes or brown and even how tall we grow. All living things have DNA, but each species is unique because of differences in their DNA. For example, humans and chimpanzees share as much as 99 percent of their DNA, but their small differences set them apart.

Likewise, every human shares 99.9 percent of their DNA with other humans. However, it's the tiny 0.1 percent variation that makes us unique. You get half your genes from each parent, making your DNA one of a kind. With only four DNA letters, there are endless combinations. So everyone is different, except in the case of identical twins, who have exactly the same DNA because they started from the same tiny egg cell.

Identical twins may share the same DNA, but each one's sense of humor and experiences are uniquely their own. Even with matching genes, life's moments create differences that make each twin's personality one of a kind.
KALI9/GETTY IMAGES

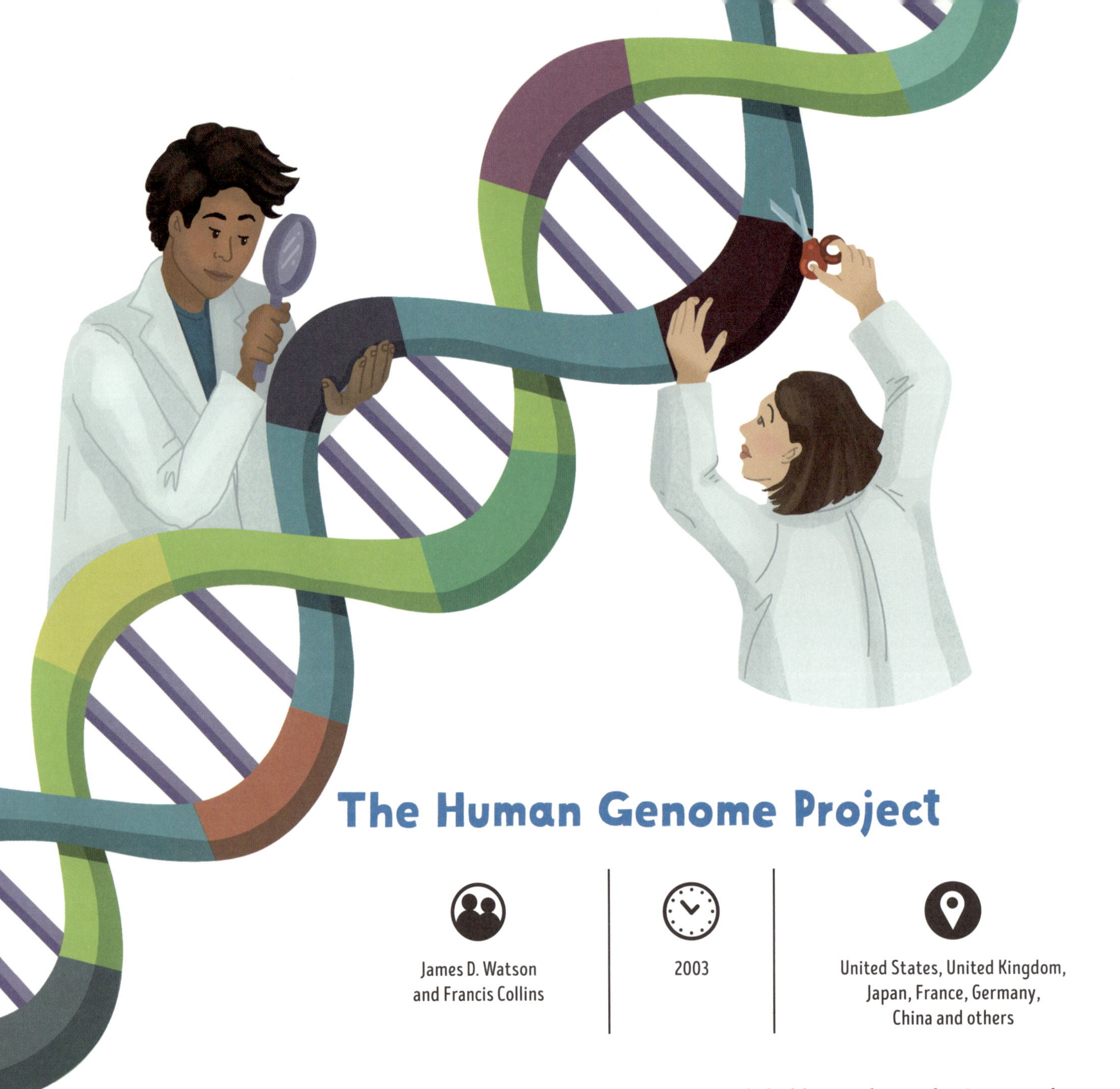

The Human Genome Project

James D. Watson and Francis Collins	2003	United States, United Kingdom, Japan, France, Germany, China and others

For a long time, our DNA was like a secret code hidden in plain sight. Scientists knew it existed and what it looked like but couldn't decipher its messages. Determined to solve this mystery, scientists launched the Human Genome Project (HGP) in 1990. Researchers around the world worked together to read the entire DNA code and understand its meaning.

Before this project began, some scientists had already studied individual genes, figuring out how they worked and what they did. However, the big question remained: How did the entire *genome* work? The genome is like a complete set of instructions for building and running a human body. The HGP researchers had a clear mission to find and map all the genes in human DNA. They wanted to understand how each gene worked. They also aimed to identify the genes linked to diseases such as cystic fibrosis, a rare inherited condition, and heart disease, a more common health issue.

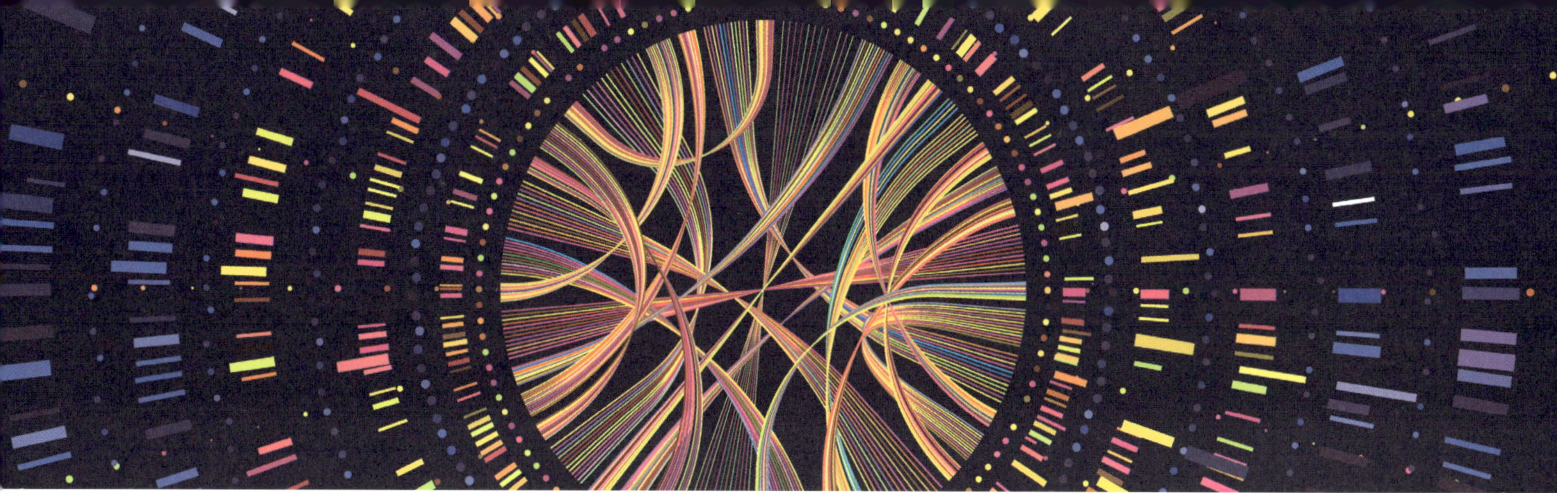

A GLOBAL CHALLENGE

Scientists began by breaking down the DNA into smaller pieces. Using computers, they sorted out which parts formed genes and which didn't. Surprisingly, genes only make up about 2 percent of the human genome. The other 98 percent was at first a mystery, often called "junk DNA." But scientists now know that it has important roles, such as controlling when and how genes work. As computer technology improved, the mapping process got faster. In 2001 the HGP scientists revealed the first draft of the complete human genome, followed by a more detailed version.

HUMAN IMPACT

The completion of the HGP in 2003 marked a major scientific achievement. But the story continues. With the genetic code cracked, scientists gained an incredible tool. They can now identify which genes are linked to different diseases. This is helping them understand inherited diseases like Tay-Sachs, sickle cell and Huntington's.

The first complete sequence of a human genome is freely available online for scientists worldwide to explore. It's like having a decoded map of how our bodies work, why diseases occur and how to make new medicines that target specific genes. Today a person's individual genome—your own genetic code with its individual variations—can be sequenced in just a few days. While this doesn't mean that every disease can be diagnosed directly, it lets scientists spot changes in genes that could lead to illness. This helps them diagnose genetic disorders more precisely and match treatments to each person's unique DNA. Scientists continue to research what certain genes do and how they are controlled.

Genome mapping is like a secret code for your body. This colorful sequence holds all the instructions that make you unique—from your hair color to how tall you'll grow.
TETIANA LAZUNOVA/GETTY IMAGES

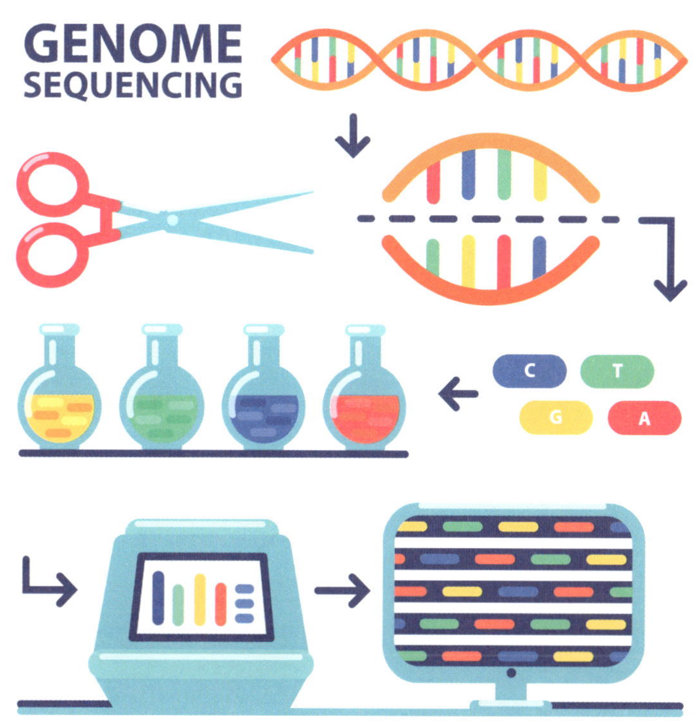

Did you know? Each cell in your body holds 3 billion DNA letters. If you stretched out the DNA from just one cell, it would be about 6.5 feet (2 meters) long—and your body has around 30 trillion cells!
MSPOINT/GETTY IMAGES

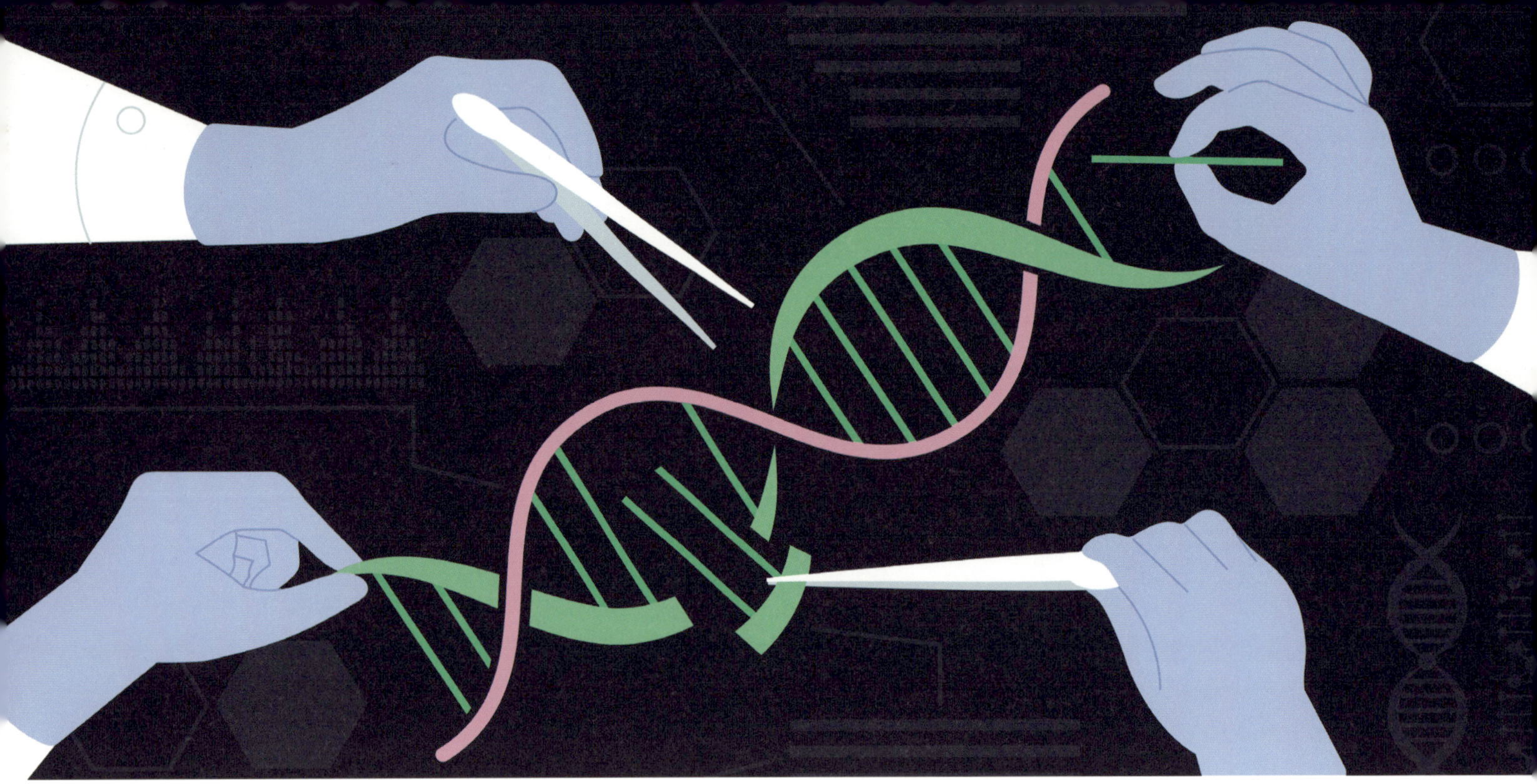

Cutting-edge science at work—scientists can now edit DNA, the building blocks of life, making small changes that could transform the future of medicine and technology.
MICROONE/SHUTTERSTOCK.COM

CRISPR

Jennifer Doudna and Emmanuelle Charpentier

2012

United States and Europe

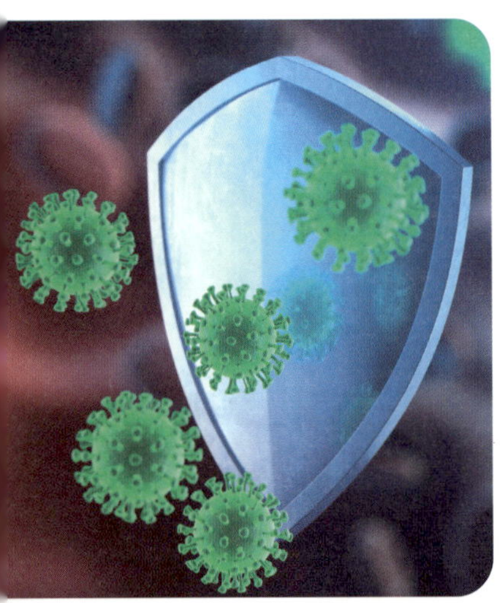
Standing guard! The immune system acts like a team of defenders, always on alert to protect our bodies from harmful invaders and keep us healthy.
CREATIVENEKO/GETTY IMAGES

CRISPR technology changes how we work with DNA. It acts like a very tiny pair of scissors. Scientists can use these scissors to snip away the bits of DNA that could cause illness and replace them with healthy ones instead. But today, its applications go way beyond just health.

In the late 1980s researchers began noticing strange repeating sequences in bacteria's DNA, but they weren't sure what these sequences did. They named them CRISPR sequences, short for clustered regularly interspaced short palindromic repeats.

Fast-forward to the early 2000s, and scientists discovered that bacteria use CRISPR to defend themselves against viruses. It turned out that CRISPRs were a family of genetic sequences found in the genomes of organisms such as bacteria as part of their ***immune system***.

When a virus (which is a tiny invader) attacks, bacteria capture a small part of the virus's DNA—kind of like taking a snapshot to remember its enemy. If the same virus tries to attack again, the bacteria produce a molecule called RNA that matches the virus's DNA from the snapshot. This RNA guides a special protein to find and cut the virus's DNA. The cut stops the virus from harming the bacteria. Scientists learned how this system works and realized they could use it to cut specific parts of DNA in other organisms, like humans.

CRISPR: TODAY AND THE FUTURE

Today CRISPR technology has transformed how we understand and interact with genes. It gives scientists a clearer picture of how genes affect our health. But its impact doesn't stop there. In farming, for example, CRISPR can be used to help make food crops tougher and more able to fight off diseases. CRISPR is also being used to develop trees that can absorb more carbon dioxide, helping to tackle climate change. Its potential is still growing.

From the first secret codes to today's genetic discoveries, coding has always been about exploring new possibilities. The adventure continues, and there are so many amazing discoveries still to come.

QUALITY STOCK ARTS/SHUTTERSTOCK.COM

DNA as Digital Storage

DNA is like nature's hard drive, storing all the instructions for life. This made scientists wonder if it could store other things, such as the digital data from our computers and phones. As we create more data every day, finding enough space to store it all is becoming a big challenge. DNA could be the answer.

Just one gram of DNA can hold a whopping 215 million gigabytes of data—nearly one million iPhones' (265 GB each) worth of storage! DNA is also incredibly compact and can last for a very long time, even thousands of years, without getting damaged.

Here's how it could work. Scientists would turn computer files, which are stored in binary code, into the language of DNA using the four letters A, G, T and C, which represent the building blocks of DNA. This would then be written and stored. To retrieve the data, the DNA would be read, and the genetic code translated back into computer code that we can read on our devices. The best part? DNA can make loads of error-free copies. DNA storage could be a big win for keeping our digital world safe and small!

GLOSSARY

adjustable—able to be changed or tweaked

aligning—falling in a row, or line

allies—groups of people or countries that work together, helping and supporting one another in an ongoing activity or effort. When capitalized as Allies, it refers to the military coalition formed during World War II to oppose Germany.

artificial intelligence—the ability of a computer program or machine to imitate human behavior such as learning, making decisions and completing tasks

binary—a number system based only on the numerals 0 and 1. Binary code is the language computers use.

brute force attack—the process of trying many passwords or codes quickly to break into a computer system

Central Intelligence Agency (CIA)—a US government agency that gathers and studies security information from around the world

codons—sets of three of the four DNA compounds that tell our bodies what to do

confidential—intended for or restricted to the use of a particular person or group; not meant for everyone to know

cryptanalysis—the solving of codes and secret messages

cyberthreats—dangers that come from the internet, like viruses or hackers

elliptical curves—sets of points that describe a curve or wave shape. The algebraic structure of these curves makes them useful for encoding information securely.

engraved—carved or etched into a surface

frequency analysis—a way to break codes by studying how often letters or groups of letters are used in a message

gene—the set of chemicals inside our cells that controls such characteristics as hair color or height. Genes are grouped together in chromosomes.

genetic—related to genes or heredity. The biological information passed down from parents to their children.

Government Code and Cypher School—a British organization that worked on breaking codes during World War II

hackers—people who use computers to get unauthorized access to data

identity theft—the illegal use of someone else's personal information without their permission in order to commit fraud

immune system—the system in our bodies that protects us from germs and other an enemy substances

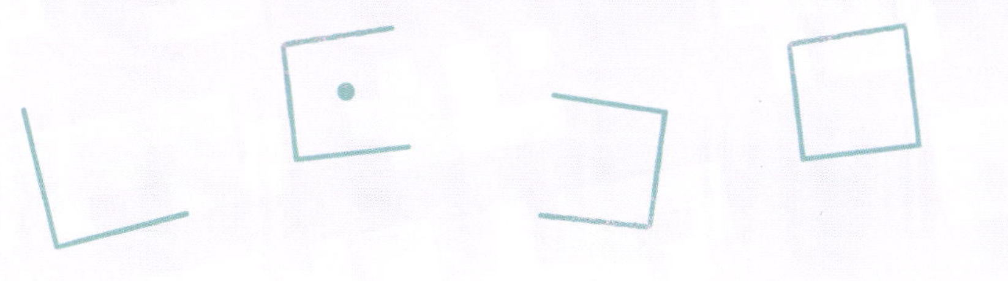

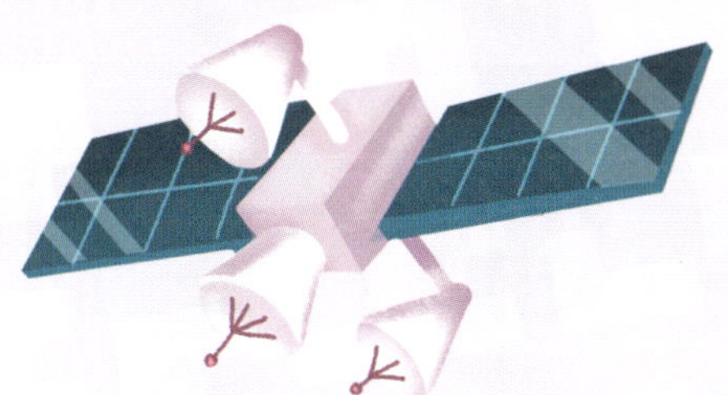

intelligence gathering—the collecting of information about what an enemy is doing or planning to do

intercepted—caught or stopped on its way from one place to another

keystream—a sequence of random letters or numbers that is combined with plaintext to encode a message

machine code—the basic language computers understand, made up of ones and zeros

malware—software designed to harm or break into a computer system

mobsters—members of organized crime groups engaged in such activities as smuggling, selling banned substances or making threats to earn money

monoalphabetic—using the letters of a single alphabet

National Security Agency (NSA)—a US government agency focused on national security and codebreaking

polyalphabetic—using multiple alphabets

random—having no specific pattern or plan

symbols—pictures or shapes that represent something else, such as emojis

tap—a device used to listen secretly to messages sent over telephone or telegraph cables

think tank—a group organized to research and solve problems

RESOURCES

Print

Daigneau, Jean. *Code Cracking for Kids: Secret Communications Throughout History, with 21 Codes and Ciphers.* Chicago Review Press, 2019.

Isaacson, Walter, with Sarah Durand. *The Code Breaker: Jennifer Doudna and the Race to Understand Our Genetic Code.* Simon & Schuster Books for Young Readers, 2022.

McKay, Sinclair. *Bletchley Park Brainteasers: The World War II Codebreakers Who Beat the Enigma Machine—And More Than 100 Puzzles and Riddles That Inspired Them.* Quercus, 2018.

Moore, Gareth. *Explorer Academy Code-Breaking Activity Adventure.* NatGeo Under the Stars, 2019.

Richardson, Michael Lee. *The Extraordinary Life of Alan Turing.* Puffin, 2020.

Roman, Carole P. *Spies, Code Breakers, and Secret Agents: A World War II Book for Kids.* Rockridge Press, 2020.

Online

Ada Lovelace: kids.nationalgeographic.com/history/article/ada-lovelace

Australian Signals Directorate 75th-anniversary 50-cent coin: abc.net.au/news/2022-09-05/how-to-solve-spy-australian-signals-directorate-50-cent-coin/101405266

Camp X: education.historicacanada.ca/en/tools/126

Code Talkers: americanindian.si.edu/static/why-we-serve/topics/code-talkers

Coding: The Next Generation: gchq.gov.uk/information/coding-the-next-generation

Cybersecurity Labs: pbs.org/wgbh/nova/labs/lab/cyber

Elizebeth Smith Friedman: womenshistory.org/education-resources/biographies/elizebeth-smith-friedman

The Gene Scene: amnh.org/explore/ology/genetics

The Home of the Codebreakers: bletchleypark.org.uk

The Story of Canada's Code Talkers: cbc.ca/kids/articles/the-story-of-canadas-code-talkers

ACKNOWLEDGMENTS

My heartfelt gratitude to the incredible team at Orca Book Publishers. A special thanks to Kirstie Hudson for her editing expertise and invaluable suggestions that helped this book take shape, and to designer Dahlia Yuen, whose wonderful creative input has left a lasting impression on every page. My sincere appreciation to Georgia Bradburne for her thoughtful insights that have touched every aspect of this book and to Meegan Lim for the beautiful illustrations that bring the words to life.

And, as always, thank you to Bas, Isla, Rose and Rhys, whose belief in the power of curiosity fuels my passion for exploring the secrets of our world. Your support means everything to me.

INDEX

*Page numbers in **bold** indicate an image caption.*

TOP SECRET

From the PAST to the PRESENT and into the FUTURE!

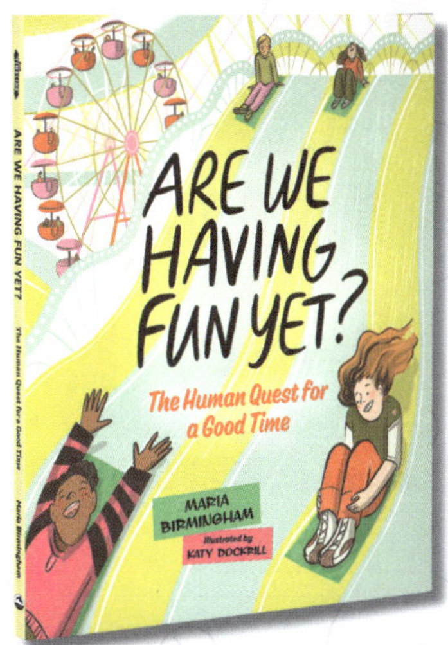

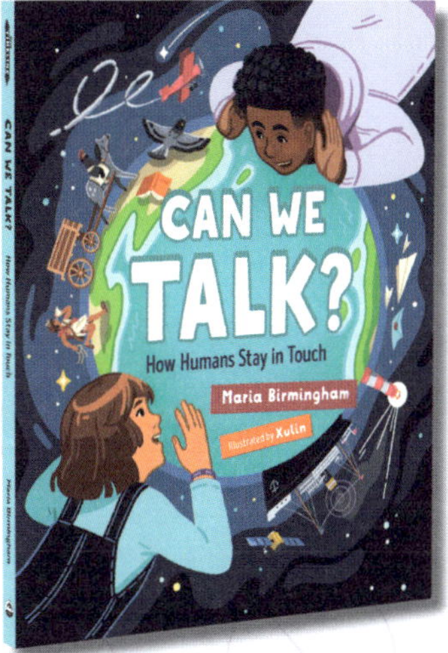

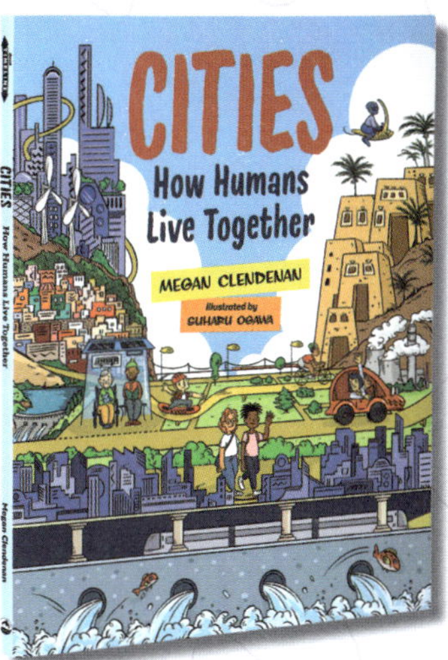

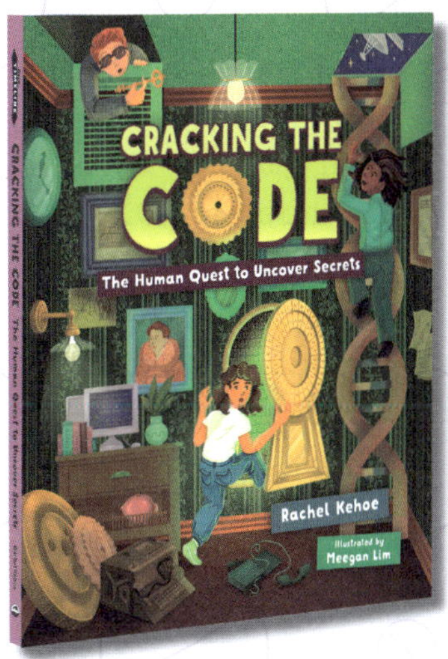

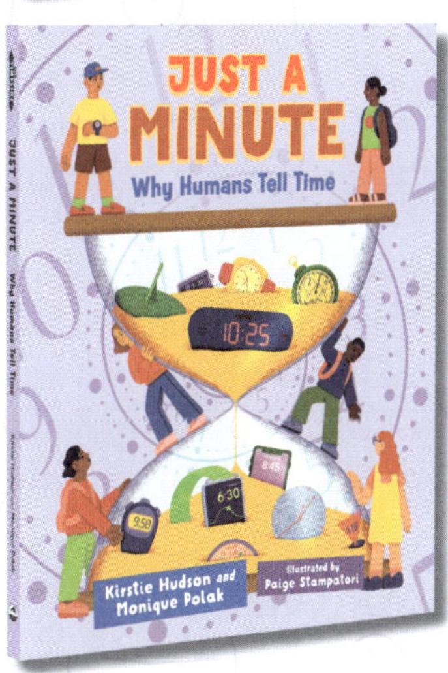

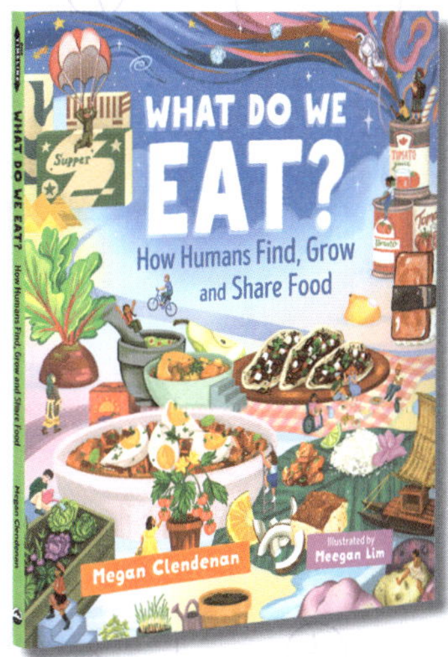

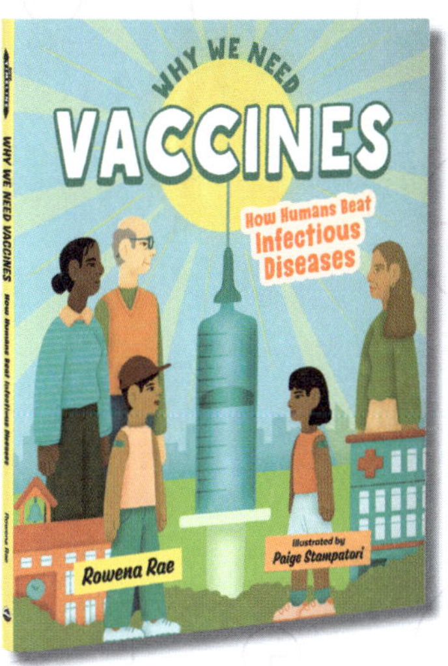

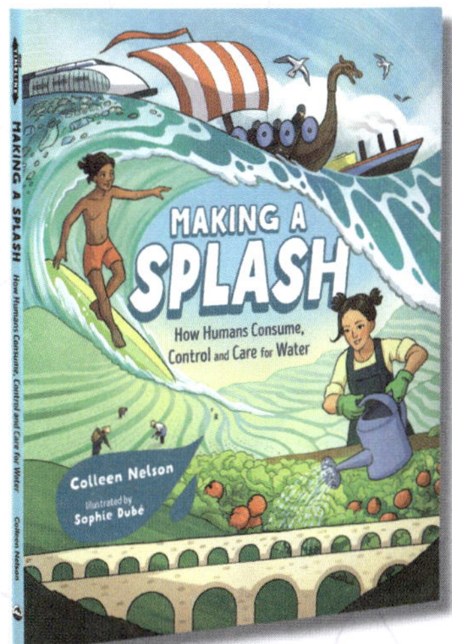

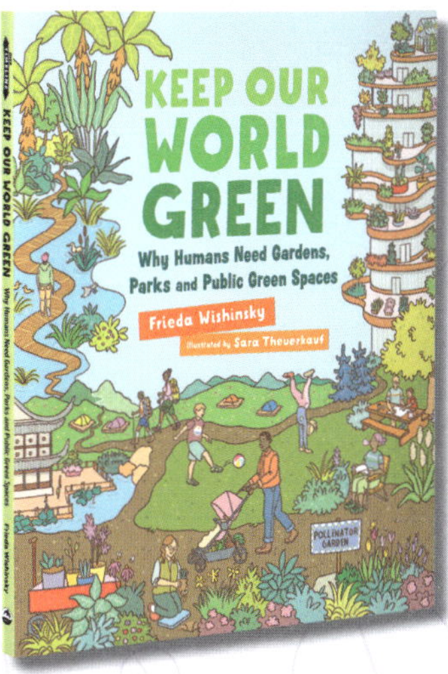

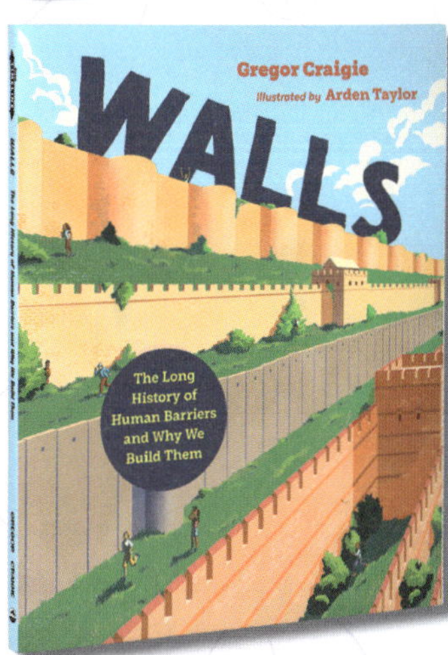

The Orca TIMELINE series explores how big ideas have shaped humanity. Discover what our collective history can tell us about the planet today and tomorrow.

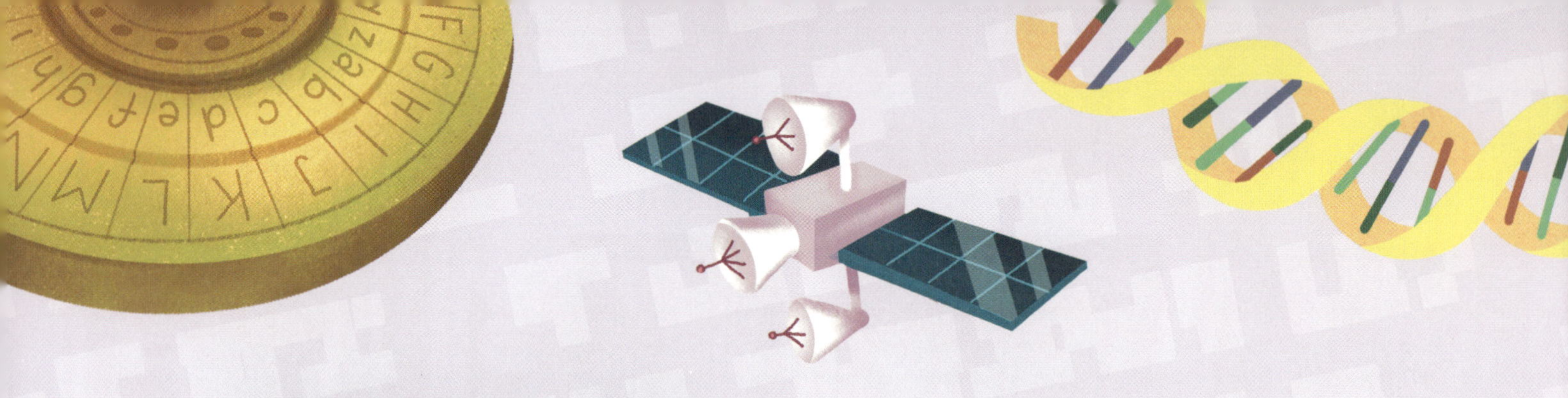

Rachel Kehoe is a Canadian nonfiction writer. She was a regular contributor to magazines such as *Muse* and *Faces,* and has also published nonfiction books on a range of topics from climate change and energy technology to artificial intelligence and mental health awareness. Rachel's book *The Trailblazing Life of Viola Desmond* is one of the top 10 titles on the 2023 Ontario Library Association's Best Bets list.

Dusty Loops

Meegan Lim is an illustrator and arts facilitator striving to nurture community growth and healing through visual arts. She holds a bachelor of design and illustration from OCAD University. Her work primarily focuses on the intersections of food and cultural identity, manifesting through detailed gouache illustrations, digital paintings and risograph zines. Her illustrations have been featured in *Chatelaine*, *Eater* and *Broken Pencil* magazines and the books *What We Talk About When We Talk About Dumplings* and *What Do We Eat?*. Meegan lives in Brampton, Ontario.

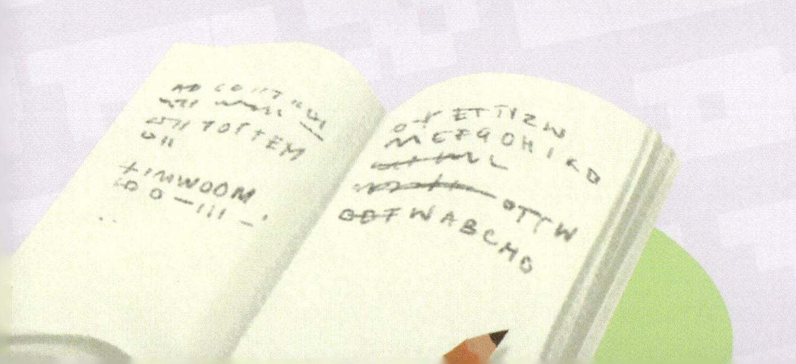